BENN'S WORLD HISTORIES

The Sick Man of Europe

Ottoman Empire to
Turkish Republic 1789–1923

CHARLES SWALLOW

ERNEST BENN/LONDON & TONBRIDGE/1973

First published 1973 by Ernest Benn Limited
Sovereign Way, Tonbridge, Kent &
25 New Street Square, Fleet Street, London EC4A 3JA

© *Charles Swallow 1973*

Maps by K. J. Wass

Book designed by Kenneth Day

Distributed in Canada by
The General Publishing Company Limited, Toronto

Printed in Great Britain

ISBN 0 510–18420–0

Title page :
1   A Turkish soldier of the nineteenth century

Contents

Maps

1 The Ottoman Empire in 1800: Symptoms of Decline

If the Ottoman Empire is still vast and extensive; . . . [none the less] in the enervating lap of sloth, the ferocious conqueror has degenerated into a torpid barbarian, whose only marks of former powers are to be traced in the insolence of his present demeanour, and the fallen affection of his fancied dignity.

IN THE EIGHTEENTH CENTURY the Ottoman Empire was in a state of rapid decay and, like France, stood in urgent need of reform. Certainly the size of the empire was daunting. In theory the Sultan ruled from the Persian Gulf to Bosnia, from the north coast of the Black Sea to Yemen, while he claimed a vague suzerainty over Algiers, Tunis, and Tripoli. The Balkan states of Moldavia and Wallachia, known as the Principalities, retained considerable independence although by tradition the Sultan appointed their *Hospodars* or rulers. Montenegro, the Morea, and even the Muslim areas of Bosnia and Albania jealously guarded their freedom, though nominally under Turkish rule. Further south, the *pashaliks* of Baghdad and Damascus had become virtually hereditary and Egypt was dominated by the Mamluk *beys*, descendants of former Circassian slaves. Nor was the Sultan more than a token ruler over large tracts of his ancient province of Anatolia. The land was infested by local chieftains, or *derebeyis*, while as a contemporary observer recorded: 'all the inhabitants of the mountains from Smyrna to Palestine are perfectly independent, and are considered by the Porte as enemies, whom they attack whenever there is an opportunity.'

The Sultans were often prevented by their upbringing from being anything but degenerate or incompetent. Confined to the seraglio, their sons grew up in the company of the women and eunuchs of the harem. It is hardly surprising that few of them after the reign of Süleyman the Magnificent had much appetite for government. An Act passed by Mehmet the Conqueror had provided that, for

5

the good of the state, Sultans should murder their brothers and ensure the peaceful succession of the throne from father to son. Murad III (1574–95) is reputed to have had 102 children of whom twenty survived him. The eldest of these ordered his slaves to strangle the remaining nineteen immediately after the burial of his father.

To prevent the appearance of a minor, an Act of 1617 decreed that the succession should go 'to the eldest surviving male member of the imperial house'; in consequence, uncles and cousins succeeded to the throne more often than sons. Incarcerated for years in the *kafes*, or cages, in the seraglio, these elderly relatives were often unsuited to rule and depositions became more frequent. While there was no attempt to establish a rival dynasty, any reforming inclinations of the Sultan usually led to his being deposed. Sultan Ahmed III (1703–30), for instance, was forced to abdicate chiefly because of the increasing European flavour of his court.

The keynote of a Sultan's upbringing was conservatism and separation from foreign influences. They had little knowledge of the world, and their studies consisted mostly of law, astrology, and official composition. Most significant of all, they had a horrified contempt for all things non-Muslim. For the Sultan was not only Emperor: he was also the Caliph or head of the Sunnite Muslim Church throughout the world. Interpretations of this title varied but broadly it was the Sultan's task to rule in accordance with the sacred law, *Sharia*, which was administered by the Sheikh-ul-Islam. There being no distinction between church and state in Islam, the sole restriction on the exercise of the Sultan's absolute authority was that it could not be contrary to religious law. The twin problem facing the nineteenth-century Sultans begins to emerge. First, their background and upbringing was narrow and confined, to say the least. But even if they broke through the barriers and sought to emulate Western customs and administrative practices, they ran up against the conservative elements of a church that traditionally regarded all things Christian as inferior.

To his people, the Sultan must have appeared a very distant and remote figure although the weapons of his autocracy must constantly have reminded them of his power. In Constantinople the Minister of Police often invaded the privacy of individual citizens. Corruption

6

Jamissaire allant a la Guerre

2 A Janissary: a member of the former *corps élite* of the Ottoman Army, whose out-of-date weapons show how they had outlived their usefulness

and bribery accompanied every transaction but few dared to draw attention to themselves by acquiring large personal fortunes. In the provinces it was impossible for the Sultan not to decentralize his power, although he pursued the traditional Turkish practice of extracting the maximum amount of tribute possible.

Beneath the Sultan was the Grand Vizier, the first Minister of the empire. He appointed prominent officials, commanded the army in

3 'An accurate reproduction of the town of Constantinople which the Turks call Istanbul

time of war, and presided over the imperial council, or *Divan*, which acted as a high court of justice. In the eighteenth century no thought of popular representation was entertained and governmental decisions were usually arrived at by the old Ottoman practice of consultation, known as *Mesveret*, among appointed officials.

Nowhere is the decline of Ottoman power more dramatically revealed than in the record of military defeats after 1683. Blocked from eastern expansion by the powerful Safavid dynasty in Persia, unable seriously to impede the southwards expansion of Russia around the Black Sea, Sultans were increasingly committed to wars in eastern Europe where their armies began to compare unfavourably with their imperial opponents. The armies of the Holy Roman Empire had begun to reap the reward of improved tactics, better weapons, and more efficient methods of supply and transport. The Turkish soldier, who in the words of Ali Pasha, writing in 1774, 'had suffered no loss of courage or morale', was but a helpless cog in an outworn military machine. The Janissaries, recruited originally from Christian boys captured by the Turks, had long since ceased to be a *corps élite*; they were now a privileged and conservative caste, more of a threat to the Sultan than to the Sultan's enemies. Symbolic of all that was

8

(1626).' Constantinople was renamed Istanbul
after its conquest by Sultan Mehmet II in 1453

reactionary and arbitrary in the rule of the Ottoman Empire, the
Janissaries had been established before the fall of Constantinople.
They were well looked after and above all well fed. The organization
of their Corps was based on the kitchen and its appliances. The Corps
itself was known as the *Ojak* (hearth), the commanding officer of a
battalion known as a 'soup-maker'. The traditional sign of revolt
was when the Janissaries overturned their soup-kettles, signifying
that they would no longer eat the Sultan's food. In time of peace,
their duties included keeping order in the towns, serving as escorts,
and guarding the principal gates of the fortresses. By the end of the
eighteenth century the Janissaries had degenerated into a lawless and
uncontrolled clique. If they disapproved of an act of government, they
had been known to set fire to the houses of Constantinople, while any
Sultan who cherished notions of reforming the Corps was liable to
find himself deposed. Furthermore, the decline of the feudal fief-
holders, or *Sipahis*, by the sixteenth century had seen a corresponding
increase in the numbers of the Janissaries.

The economy of the Ottoman Empire had suffered too. The
monetary crisis caused by the sudden influx of American gold and
silver in the sixteenth century had coincided with the decline of the

Sipahis. By debasement and devaluation, the government had sought vainly to pay for an increasingly mercenary army as well as a top-heavy bureaucracy. Officialdom ran riot. Tax-farmers took over the lands and the standard of husbandry went down. Foreign trade was based largely on the export of raw materials such as silk, wool, and cotton to western Europe in return for manufactured articles such as ironware, clocks, and paper. By a system of Capitulations, foreign merchants at ports such as Constantinople and Smyrna were free from Turkish control and had begun to sell this privilege to Ottoman subjects. These privileges were both judicial and commercial and through the Capitulations foreign powers had over the years built up considerable holdings on Turkish soil. France had obtained her first Capitulations in 1536, England in 1580, and other countries followed. At first, these important advantages had been granted by Sultans in the plentitude of their power and to save them the trouble of bothering about the cases of unimportant foreign Christians. Later on, however, as the foreigners benefited from the privileges, they came to be seen as an intolerable affront to Turkish nationalism.

The Ottoman Empire had been fashioned by Islam. The early Ottomans had been converted in the tenth century and their's was a militant, frontier faith. Osman (1288–1326), the conqueror from whom his Turkish subjects took their historic name of Ottoman, rejoiced in the title of 'Sultan, son of the Sultan of the Ghazis, Ghazi, Son of the Ghazi . . . marchlord of the horizons, hero of the world'. The Muslim concept of Holy War (*jihad*) waged by Ghazis, special champions of the Faith, was channelled into a war first against Byzantium and then against western Christendom. But by the eighteenth century, the soldiers of Islam were in retreat. The proselytizing zeal of early days had been replaced by the rigid conservatism of the Ulema, a class of religious leaders and teachers. The early Sultans had effectively fused the *Sharia* into the system of law and government; but their achievement was to paralyse the limbs of the Ottoman state. No less disastrous was the Millet system, by which individual, non-Muslim communities, isolated from each other and enjoying different social, political, and economic privileges, were weakly linked through an ecclesiastical administration. In a sense the Millet system was the religious counterpart to the Capitulations. It pointed to the comprehensive nature of the Ottoman State which although Islamic in

4 Sipahi. This majestic figure was not unlike
the medieval knight of feudal England, although
he held his land temporarily in return for military service

character was to some extent also Christian. A Millet meant a community and the most important of these were the Greek Orthodox, the Armenians, and the Jews. Useful bases for intrigues by the Great Powers later on, the Millets began as examples of Ottoman tolerance born of expediency.

MAP NO. I
The Ottoman Empire in 1800

The failure of Kara Mustapha, the Grand Vizier, and his Turkish army to take Vienna in 1683 marked a turning-point in the history of south-east Europe. It was the prelude to a series of military reverses suffered by the Turks during the eighteenth century. In 1774 at Kutchuk-Kainardji, a small village in Bulgaria, the new Sultan, Abdul Hamid I (1774–89), was forced by the Empress of Russia, Catherine II, to sign an ignominious treaty by which he renounced not only conquered lands inhabited by Christians but also old Muslim territory in the Crimea. Poised between Christendom and Islam, the Ottoman Empire lay ripe for partition. To the north and west were her Christian neighbours, Russia and Austria; while within her southern boundaries there lived the fiercely independent Muslims, the Mamluks of Egypt.

The call for reform at Constantinople coincided with the outbreak of the French revolution but was inspired by very different motives. The French demands for social and political equality were not shared by the Turk. True, the almost medieval form of government at the Porte was as grossly out of date as the *ancien régime* presided over by Louis XVI. Turkish resentment, however, was directed not so much against the blatant corruption of the rulers as against the infidel. Süleyman the Magnificent, the heroic sixteenth-century Sultan, although in 1565 a dying man, had nevertheless dragged himself away from the comfort of his seraglio to wage with evangelical fervour one final campaign in Hungary against the Hapsburg Emperor, Maximilian II. Such a spirit of mission was lacking in the eighteenth century. Instead, both Sultan and Turk had become morbidly introspective and military defeats were set against the backcloth of a tottering governmental machine and widespread corruption. Some small concessions to reform had been made but the European enlightenment had passed by largely unnoticed in the Ottoman Empire. There was little intellectual stimulus in Constantinople. Not until 1727 was the first printing-press set up – and that by a renegade Hungarian. Before its closure, fifteen years later, the press had printed only seventeen books. Count de Bonneval, a French nobleman who arrived in Constantinople in 1729, instigated reforms in the army; while in 1773, another Frenchman, Baron de Tott, organized a new school of mathematics for the navy.

Sultan Selim III (1789–1808) translated the recognized need for reform into fact. He leant heavily on French military knowledge in preparing his New Order for the armed forces, the *Nizam-i Cedid*. Twenty-two imperial dignitaries offered proposals for reform but it was towards the radicals among them who wanted an army reorganized upon European lines that the Sultan himself inclined. Military and naval schools were set up, French officers recruited as teachers, and the French language became compulsory for students. In 1796, the French Ambassador, General Aubert Dubayet, arrived in Constantinople accompanied by a group of French military experts. Even after the French occupation of Egypt (1798–1802), General

Sebastiani managed to restore the pattern of French military co-operation during his mission in 1806–7. Predictably, Selim III's military reforms earned the opposition of the Janissaries. In 1807 partisans of reform were dragged to the Hippodrome and slaughtered, while the Janissary officers enforced the abolition of the *Nizam-i Cedid* and deposed the Sultan.

Short-lived though the military reforms proved to be, Selim III's New Order included a general programme of reform, the effects of which were to live after him. In 1792 he had established permanent Ottoman embassies in the chief European capitals and it was not long before the secretariats of these new embassies were staffed with young Turks anxious to absorb Western ideas. The Sultan instructed his ambassadors to study the institutions of the countries to which they were sent and also to acquire 'languages, knowledge, and sciences useful to servants of the empire'.

Within his own empire, the Sultan had drawn up new regulations concerning provincial taxation, governorships, control of the grain trade, and other administrative matters. In short, he had opened up channels of communication with the West and if, as one Turkish historian has put it, 'the scientific current broke against the dikes of literature and jurisprudence', at least some of the ideas from an enlightened Europe were starting to filter through. There may have been more than a trace of irony in the solemn ceremony in 1793 when Citizen Déscorches (*ci-devant* Marquis de Sainte-Croix) planted a tree of liberty in the soil of Turkey; but there was no denying that some of the ideas of the French revolutionaries had been implanted in Ottoman minds.

The imperial historiographer, Ahmed Asim Effendi, wrote a chronicle of the years 1791–1808 in which he berates the French, whose republic he describes as 'the rumblings and crepitations of a queasy stomach'. Fervently anti-Christian himself, Asim recognized the value of borrowing the sciences and techniques of the West, as Russia had done a century before. He had little use, however, for French revolutionary dogma – 'the abandonment of religion and the equality of rich and poor':

Certain sensualists, naked of the garment of loyalty, from time to time learned politics from them; some desirous of learning their language,

5　Selim III (1789–1808), the Sultan who
recognized the need to drag his empire out of
the torpor of the eighteenth century

took French teachers, acquired their idiom and prided themselves ... on
their uncouth talk.

Despite Asim's dire warnings, the educated Ottoman could now
open his mind to the new ideas from France without fear of religious
contamination. Probably most Ottomans thought of the French as
useful technical advisers and no more; but already the principles
of popular representation and corporate decision were being seriously
discussed by thoughtful Turks. As the nineteenth century began to
unfold, such ideas were to take concrete form in the movement for
national sovereignty.

The weakness of the Ottoman Empire did not go unnoticed by the
countries of northern Europe. In the days before the French revolution it was the threat of Catherine II of Russia that most alarmed the
Turks. It was no secret that she dreamed of forming a Greek empire
at Constantinople, to be conferred on her infant grandson. Medals

6   Nelson's victory over the French off the
mouth of the Nile cut Napoleon's lifeline to the
Levant and ruined his chance of dominating the East

had already been struck depicting the destruction of the Mosque
at Constantinople by lightning. Her more sober aims included
strengthening Russian control of the Crimea, the development of
Russian Black Sea trade based on the newly founded port of Kherson,
and a penetration of the eastern littoral of the Black Sea under the
pretext of protecting the Orthodox Christians in the Principalities.
In the Russo-Turkish War of 1788–92, Russia advanced at the expense
of Turkey while the rest of Europe turned a blind eye or salvaged
what they could from the spoils. At Jassy in 1792, Catherine demanded that the Russian boundary be extended to the river Dniester;
at the same time all existing agreements between Russia and the Porte
were confirmed. As Catherine paused to take stock of recent events in
France, the Sultan had little time to lick his wounds before being
faced by a fresh attack upon the southern borders of his empire.

With the exception of France, the countries of western Europe had only a tenuous contact with the Ottoman Empire. Spain regarded the Muslims as her natural enemy and had no diplomatic relations with the Porte before 1783. Britain possessed waning commercial links through the Levant Company, but the Ottomans were not an important factor in British foreign policy for most of the eighteenth century. France, however, had a long standing connection with the Ottomans dating back to the reign of Francis I (1515–47). Indeed, she had come to look upon the Ottomans as a useful stick with which to belabour the Austrians in the east and divert Hapsburg interest from the Rhine. The Sultan regarded the King of France as a reliable ally and the French enjoyed a favourable position at the Porte.

By the time of Napoleon, the Franco-Turkish alliance had become virtually meaningless. Military and technical aid was still sent to Constantinople. Indeed, Napoleon had written a letter to his brother Joseph in 1795 saying that he might go 'with a flattering ambassadorial title to organize the artillery of the Grand Turk'. More realistically, the Directory soon accepted that there was little they could do but offer token support for Turkish resistance to Russia. There was, therefore, an indisputable logic about Napoleon's decision to embark upon his Egyptian campaign. In a memorandum to the Directory in 1798, he had written, 'the time is not distant when we shall realize that to destroy England we must take possession of Egypt'. The immediate political aim of the expedition was to drive the English from the Orient and cut off their trade routes with India. Napoleon's lame attempt at justifying French action was that the Mamluk *beys* had 'formed most intimate ties with the English'. The horrified reaction of the Porte came as a surprise to him, since he had calmly supposed that the Sultan would have little objection as Egypt had been virtually independent of Turkish rule for some time. Perhaps the Porte was more worried by the rising prices of rice and coffee caused by the French invasion of Egypt than by the blow to her self-esteem. At any rate, by 2 September 1798, the French chargé d'affaires, Ruffin, had been committed to the Seven Towers and a week later the Porte declared war on France.

Napoleon's invasion of Egypt, besides upsetting the Turks, was a strategic failure. The spectacular victory of the French over the Mamluk army at the Battle of the Pyramids (21 July 1798), where 18,000

Muslims managed to kill a mere 30 Frenchmen was more than undone by the annihilation of the French fleet by Nelson at the Battle of the Nile (1 August 1798). Napoleon, cut off by the loss of his fleet from French reinforcements, was now confronted by an Anglo-Turkish alliance bent on expelling him from the Levant. Russia, too, no friend of the revolution, had agreed to reinforce the Turkish navy in the Mediterranean by a formal alliance signed on 3 January 1799. A secret clause of this treaty, with important implications for the future, gave Russian warships the right of passage through the Straits and sole responsibility for their defence; it was also stated that no warships other than those of Russia and Turkey should enter the Black Sea. Meanwhile Napoleon had made his strange decision to invade Syria but was checked at Acre by a Turkish force supported by a British squadron under Sir Sydney Smith. Despite French victories over the Turks and the British at Aboukir and Heliopolis, Napoleon had given Egypt up for lost by August 1799 when he returned to France. Three months later, the remaining French forces surrendered to the British.

The transparent insincerity of the Sultan's new-found allies was revealed by Britain's unwillingness to support direct Ottoman rule over the Mamluks in Egypt and Russian reluctance to give up effective control of the Ionian Islands, captured from the French by a Russo-Turkish fleet in 1799. The British were becoming more and more alarmed at the prospect of growing Russian interest in the Ottoman Empire; they were anxious too that the Tsar should not be persuaded by his advisers to ignore Napoleon and concentrate on the East. Tsar Alexander I (1801–25), anxious to check the build-up of French influence in the eastern Mediterranean, gradually swung towards an artificial alliance with Britain and Turkey.

So flimsy a union could not possibly withstand the shockwaves set up in Constantinople by Napoleon's victories at Ulm and Austerlitz. Quick to seize the chance, Napoleon dispatched General Sebastiani to Constantinople in 1806 to woo the Turks with the offer of French help to recover the Crimea. So it came as no surprise when Turkey declared war on Russia in 1806 after the Tsar, alarmed at the evidence of French influence at the Porte, had sent a Russian army into the Principalities. Meanwhile Britain, unable to dislodge the French from Constantinople despite the efforts of her navy, was by the summer

7   Sultan Mahmud II, who saw the need to
Westernize the army and the cumbersome
Ottoman bureaucracy

of 1807 forced out of Egypt too. The diplomatic revolution, implicit
in the Tilsit agreement of 1807 between Napoleon and Alexander,
must have caused consternation in both London and Constantinople.
Still, the meeting between the two Emperors at Erfurt in the following
year probably dispelled their worst fears, for by then Napoleon's
expansive schemes for Turkish partition and a combined Franco-
Russian attack on India had evaporated as he came to be preoccupied
with Spain.

The deposition of Sultan Selim III in 1807 was effected by the

Janissaries who had opposed his reforms. A palace revolution ensued, the outcome of which was that Mahmud II, the sole surviving male member of the Ottoman dynasty, became Sultan in 1808. Besides the blatant weaknesses of the Ottoman State itself, the reign of Selim III had seen the beginnings of agitation for independence in three separate areas of the empire. In 1804 the Serbs had risen in revolt; in 1806 Mohammed Ali, Pasha of Egypt, expelled the British and cleared the ground for independent rule; finally, the Greeks had been quick to seize upon disputes between France and Russia over influence in the Balkans to further their own movement towards independence. The combination of weak Ottoman rule and the liberating message of the French revolution started a landslide of revolt that gathered momentum as the nineteenth century dawned. It was only after the dust had settled more than a century later that a new Turkey emerged.

2 Alarum in the Balkans: The Serbian and Greek Revolts

THE GREEK REVOLT against Turkish rule in 1821, although perhaps the most celebrated, was not the first attempt by a subject people to challenge Ottoman rule. Further north in the Balkan peninsula there lay the comparatively inaccessible state of Serbia; it was here that the first spark of independence from the Porte was lit. Serbia, now part of Yugoslavia, abuts onto Hungary in the north and Wallachia in the east. Geography indicated that the Serbs should look for support in their struggle from the two major powers behind Hungary and Wallachia, namely Austria and Russia. Unhappily for Serbia, it was just this dependence during the nineteenth century on one or other of these Great Powers that lessened her chances of building up the independence so expensively bought from Constantinople.

The Serbian revolt began not as a spontaneous nationalist uprising but as a protest against the tyranny of the Janissaries. These 'masterful pretorians' had dominated the *pashalik* of Belgrade until the 1790s when their incursion across the Hungarian frontier caused Sultan Selim III to withdraw them from Serbia. Many, however, remained nearby, offering their services to the rebellious chieftain of Vidin, Pasvan Oglu. Meanwhile, for five years Serbia was wisely administered by an enlightened but firm Pasha, Hajji Mustapha, who rebuilt the churches and encouraged trade. But when he used the Serbian *Rayahs* (Christians) to withstand fresh attacks from Pasvan Oglu in 1798 and 1799, the Sultan misguidedly allowed the Janissaries to return and restore order. Their methods were characteristic. In 1801 they assassinated the Pasha and some senior Serbian officers and invited Muslims from Albania and Bosnia to come and share the spoils of Serbia. After the benevolent rule of Hajji Mustapha this open affront to Serbian national and religious sentiment provoked an anguished appeal from the local Christian magistrates to the Sultan: 'Art thou still our Tsar? Then come and free us from these evil doers . . .' Sultan Selim's ambiguous reply was to transform a local insurgence into a full-scale national revolt. He warned the Janissary leaders that he would send an army against them, 'but not an Ottoman army, for it would be a grievous thing to cause true believers to fight against each other; but soldiers should come against them of other nations. and of another creed'. The Janissaries concluded that the Sultan could only be referring to the Serbs: 'By Allah, he means the *Rayahs!*' They promptly retired to their districts and prepared to slaughter the whole Christian population in Serbia. In February 1804 the Janissaries struck; but the Serbs were now ready for them and in Karageorge they had found a national leader.

Religion too played its part in fomenting Serbian national feeling. For years the *Rayahs* had been made to suffer slights not only from the Janissaries but also the Muslim Spaki landowners. The high road to honours was to profess Islam, and it became proverbial that one must be the son of a Christian renegade to attain to the highest dignities of the Turkish Empire. Thus the 'Turks' who tried to repress the incipient uprisings in Serbia and later in Greece were often converts to Islam. They showed too that the zeal of the convert often exceeds that of the born believer. The Christians in Serbia, apart from a smattering of Roman Catholics, were all classed as Greeks, owning as they did the spiritual authority of the Oecumenical Patriarch.

With its rugged, mountainous terrain, Serbia has always had its bandits and it was from these, or the *Heyducs*, as they were called, that there emerged a number of real leaders, some of whom became national heroes. Karageorge (Black George) was the son of a Serbian peasant. A pig-dealer by profession, he took to the mountains when the Janissaries imposed themselves and, dressed always in his old herdsman's garb and black cap, he quickly made a name for himself among the *Heyducs*. When offered the leadership of the Serbs, he said: 'I am too hasty of mood for the office . . . I shall be inclined to kill at once.' To this came the sharp reply that 'such severity is needed at this time'.

The initial success of the Serbian revolt was partly the result of Karageorge's ability to unite his followers against the Janissaries and it was partly bred from the prevarications of the Sultan. With Austrian support, Karageorge was able to defeat the Janissaries, the heads of their leaders subsequently being displayed in the Serbian camp. Selim, having achieved his aim of reducing the Janissaries, naïvely

22

assumed that the Serbs would now return to their herds. Far from this, they demanded, this time with Russian support, further concessions from the Sultan, namely the garrisoning of all fortresses with Serbian troops and the waiving of all arrears of taxes and tributes because of Serbian suffering during the war. Selim, pressed by both France and Russia, gambled on a quick knock-out blow to rid himself of this minor irritation. He arrested the Serbian emissaries and ordered Afiz, the Pasha of Nissa, to invade Serbia and disarm the *Rayahs*. The Serbs resisted to a man and when Russia declared war on the Porte in 1806, Selim was forced to grant a measure of independence to Serbia. After Selim was deposed, the Tsar began to extend his 'paternal' protection to Serbia – an ominous portent. At the Treaty of Bucharest (1812), Russia, intent upon acquiring Bessarabia, was ready to forsake her ally, Serbia. Although the Serbs were granted a full amnesty and permitted to regulate their internal affairs, their fortresses were once again to be occupied by Turkish garrisons. At this Karageorge lost his nerve and fled to Austria.

The final chapter of the Serbian revolt centres round another former herdsman, Milosh Obrenovich. He was twenty years younger than Karageorge and at first less violent. Still, in 1815 he was prompted by further Turkish atrocities to resist, and on Palm Sunday, under the oak before the church at Takovo, he and his followers swore to bury their differences and unite against the common foe. Sultan Mahmud (1808–39) was forced to temper his counter-attack for fear of its effect on the members of the Holy Alliance. Two years later Karageorge returned and tried to incite Milosh to join him in an anti-Turkish revolt in the Morea. Milosh was not one to share his glory and instead he ordered the Mayor of Semendria to execute Karageorge and send his head to the Sultan.

So with much shedding of blood, a measure of independence was won for Serbia. The Turks delayed implementing the terms of agreements previously made at Akkermann (1826) and Adrianople (1829), but by a *Firman*, or decree, of 1830, although the Turks still garrisoned the Serbian fortresses, Milosh was granted the title of Hereditary Prince and the Serbs could choose their own bishops. Although still a vassal state under the suzerainty of Turkey and therefore subject to tribute, Serbia had achieved the local autonomy she sought.

23

Compared with the Serbian revolt, the Greek uprising was a more basic attack on the integrity of the Ottoman Empire. It is tempting to suppose that the impoverished Greeks, inspired by their classical heritage and helped by European sympathizers, rose up against their Turkish overlords, overthrew them, and created modern Greece. Then, as now, the confusion of interests and motives combined to create a more complex story.

Since the fall of Constantinople in 1453, Greeks could be found living throughout the whole of Turkey in Europe – in Constantinople, the Principalities, on the numerous islands round the Balkan Peninsula, and on the mainland itself. But, more and more, the Greeks on the mainland had become the victims of the conflict between East and West. Expected on the one hand to support the *jihad* of the Turks against the Christian Venetians in the Peloponnese (the Morea), the Greeks were also subject to pressure from Western Powers who chose to use them in furthering their own designs on the Turks. They tended, therefore, to seek refuge under the protective Ottoman umbrella. This state of affairs, though less than ideal for the Greeks, afforded them a certain security and they enjoyed a *de facto* independence within the empire. Why then did they revolt?

In the first place, there was a lack of direction from Constantinople. As successive Sultans, with few exceptions, withdrew from the day-to-day business of administration, so the corruption of the Janissaries and the provincial governors became more pronounced. Brigands abounded in the Greek mountains and the policemen appointed to subdue them were often little more than rival brigands. Little security existed for the ordinary Greek and, for the more educated, the contrast between their system and the more enlightened West was alarming.

Contact with the West was extending rapidly, particularly through trade:

> Levadia and Athens . . . supplied sailcloth for the Ottoman navy. English ships already visited the Morea and Messolonghi to load currants and often bought back rich scarfs, sashes of variegated silk and gold tissue, and Turkey leather of the brightest dyes, which were manufactured in different towns in Greece, particularly at Pastras, Gastouni and Lepanto.[1]

[1] George Finlay, History of Greece, vol. v

MAP NO. 2
Serbia, *c.* 1830

By the late eighteenth century Greek merchants were trading regularly with the Russians in the Black Sea and the merchant colonies at Marseilles and Leghorn in the Mediterranean. In the Napoleonic Wars, Greeks were to be found both in the French and British navies. Gradually, the ideas of revolutionary Europe began to filter through into Greece. As they became more prosperous, so the Greeks of the islands and the ports began to question Turkish rule.

The first revolt against the Turks occurred in the Peloponnese in

1770. Here the prosperity of the seafaring Greeks was not shared by those tied to the land, of which the Turks owned eighteen times as much as the Greeks. But land hunger served to unite both rich and poor in a common cause. In Russia, Catherine the Great, with her dreams of conquest around the Black Sea, was quick to exploit Greek unrest and accordingly dispatched her current lover, Count Gregory Orlov, to foment disaffections among the Greeks. The rebellion itself was a failure. Not surprisingly the Greeks and Russians had little unity of purpose. The Sultan employed the services of Ali Pasha of Jannina, whose Albanian troops put down the revolt with savage ferocity. Catherine cut her losses and left the Greeks to fend for themselves. No doubt she fondly imagined that by securing at the Treaty of Kutchuk-Kainardji (1774) the vague right to protect the Sultan's Christian subjects, she had earned their gratitude. It is more probable that the revolt opened Greek eyes to Russia's real intentions. They had learnt that Russian suzerainty was no better than that of the Sultan; the only answer was to be bound to no one.

It is always difficult to assess the effect of ideas on a revolutionary movement but it is certain that educated Greeks, particularly those living in western Europe, were influenced by the liberal ideals of the French and American revolutions. There were, too, the romantics like Byron who dreamed 'that Greece might still be free' and Rhigas Pheraios, put to death by the Turks in 1798, whose War Hymn proclaimed: 'better an hour of life that is free than forty years in slavery.' Such thoughts generated a feeling of national consciousness although at first there was a marked division between the educated Greeks of the Principalities, who still looked to Russia for help and who sought only to substitute Greek for Turkish rule within the empire, and the peasant extremists in the Peloponnese who hoped to build a new nation. It was among the former that there sprang up in 1814 a Greek society called the 'Philiki Etaireia', which was responsible for starting the Greek revolt. In 1821 one of their number, Prince Alexander Ypsilantis, crossed the river Pruth with 3,000 men, many of them Russians. The army was summarily defeated by a Turkish force and Ypsilantis promptly fled to Austria. The Sultan quickly re-established control in the Principalities and the Philiki Etaireia was forgotten. But by keeping alive the idea of Greek independence after the Congress of Vienna in 1815, when the Great

Powers looked with suspicion on any nationalist revolt, the society managed to inspire the Greeks themselves and attract the support of European Philhellenes.

On 26 April 1821, Germanós, the Metropolitan of Patras, raised the sacred banner representing the death of the Virgin, in the church of the monastery of Hagia Lávra. This was the legendary call for the Greeks to revolt but already fighting had broken out between Greek and Turk. In the Peloponnese, the garrison of Kalamata had fallen and a popular song demanded that 'not a Turk should remain in the Morea'. In June, Ypsilantis's brother, Demetrios, arrived in the Peloponnese and the Sultan was confronted too by the rebellious Ali Pasha of Jannina who wanted to extend his own rule in north-west Greece. The Sultan at once ordered the massacre of the Greeks living in Constantinople, including the Greek Patriarch himself. The venerable Gregory V, a native of the Peloponnese, was hung on Easter Sunday from the gate of his palace, publicly displayed for

8 The romance and indignation that inspired the Greek uprising are captured in this picture of Germanós, raising the standard of revolt in 1821

three days, and then dragged by the Jews (the age-old enemies of Hellenism) to the sea. At the beginning of the war Turkish atrocities of this kind were more than matched by tales of Greek cruelty. Finlay, describing the capture of Tripolitsa, the key to control of the Peloponnese writes:

> Women and children were frequently tortured before they were murdered. After the Greeks had been in possession of the city for forty-eight hours, they deliberately collected together about two thousand persons of every age and sex, but principally women and children; and led them to a ravine in the nearest mountain, where they murdered every soul.

Both sides knew they could expect no quarter if they lost, so the battles were fought with a passionate intensity.

The reaction of the Great Powers to these sporadic uprisings can have given the Greeks little cause for hope. Europe after Napoleon was distinctly hostile towards wars of liberation. Russia alone might have been expected to help an enemy of the Ottoman Empire. But far from making capital out of the Sultan's embarrassment, Tsar Alexander I was obsessed with his mystic dreams of a Holy Alliance. Together with Austria and Prussia he was to use the alliance as an instrument for the suppression of all liberal ideas. Metternich, the Austrian Minister, was terrified that the Greek revolt would open the door to Russian infiltration into the Ottoman Empire. He talked of the revolt as 'a firebrand thrown by the radicals between the Great Powers and especially between Austria and Russia'. The Great Powers, gathered at Laibach in 1821, roundly condemned the Greeks and clearly hoped that the candle of revolt would be snuffed out at once. Even in England, where liberal ideas received a more friendly reception, Canning, whose statue now stands in Athens, was not prepared to stand by the Greeks in 1821. It is easy to sympathize with the motives of a Europe that had been ravaged for twenty years by a war that had started for supposedly liberal ideals.

The final influence upon the course of the war was the make-up of Greece itself. Though small, Greece has the longest coastline of any country in Europe except Norway. Surrounded by islands, the Greeks had always been a fine seafaring people whereas the Turkish navy had less ingenuity and enterprise. The failure of the Turks

28

9 Kolokotrones, one of the Greek leaders, who
made little impression against Ibrahim Pasha in
the campaign of 1825

to win control of the sea was to be an important element in their
defeat. Not only this, but the terrain of Greece itself worked to the
disadvantage of the Turks. Three-quarters of the country is dominated by virtually impassable mountains and nearly all the towns of

any importance are situated on the coast. The Pindus mountain range divides the northern half of the country into eastern and western Rumelia; in the south, the Peloponnese peninsula is cut off from Rumelia by the Gulf and Isthmus of Corinth. It was in these three separate theatres that war on the mainland was fought and the problem for the Turks of maintaining supply-lines and communication needs no emphasizing.

Despite these natural advantages, the Greeks were very much the under-dogs in 1821. They lacked unity of leadership, clear political aims, and foreign support. Their achievement of independence in 1832 is thus all the more remarkable. The story of the fighting itself can be quickly told. The first phase lasted from 1821 to 1825 when Ibrahim Pasha, the son of Mehemet Ali, the ruler in Egypt, landed on the Peloponnese peninsula in answer to the Sultan's call for help. Military honours during this first period were roughly even though the Turks had gained the upper hand by 1825. The terrible massacre in the Turkish capital of the Peloponnese on 5 October 1821, when 8,000 Muslims were said to have perished, was more than matched

10 A German print of the capture of Messalonghi by Ibrahim Pasha in 1825

by the slaughter of thousands of Greeks on the Island of Chios the next year. Ironically, of the few who escaped, some went to Syra and founded there the industry of 'Turkish delight'. The year 1822 saw an invasion by the Turks from east and west. In the west the Turks won at Peta and in the same year they took Athens. By 1823, the Sultan was free of his war in Persia and could now devote his full attention to the Greeks. Thessaly was subdued but further south the Greeks recovered Corinth. The arrival of Lord Byron at Messalonghi in 1824 focused English attention on the Greek problem, for his name was closely linked with the Philhellenic movement in Europe. The practical value of the Greek loan raised by the London Greek Committee may have been minimal, but sympathy for the Greeks was aroused. With the landing of Ibrahim Pasha, the tide began to turn in favour of the Turks. Kolokotrones was unable to check Ibrahim in the south, while the fall of Messalonghi to the Egyptian in 1825 was crowned by the Turkish capture of Athens in June 1826. Greece was again in Turkish hands.

Victory was to elude the Sultan. In 1827, Admiral Codrington commanding a combined English, French, and Russian fleet annihilated the Egyptian-Turkish fleet at Navarino Bay.

Fate had stepped in and altered in one blow the course of the war. Locked in the Bay of Navarino, the Turkish-Egyptian fleet unwittingly provoked the Great Power fleet when a Turkish ship opened fire on one of the English boats commanded by Fitzroy. De Rigny, the French Admiral, may have claimed that 'c'est un malheureux coup tiré par les Turcs qui a engagé l'affaire', but there was little hesitation by the French and Russians in setting about the enemy. The allies lost but one ship; the Turkish-Egyptian fleet lost sixty. Codrington had some explaining to do after the battle, for hitherto Britain had followed a policy of preserving a balance of power in the eastern Mediterranean and not allowing the Turks to be humiliated. Wellington described the battle as 'an untoward event' but as a soldier he could not fail to appreciate its military significance. Now that they no longer controlled the sea, the Turks could do little to prevent Greek independence and British policy moved decisively in an anti-Russian direction through fear of Tsarist designs on the Ottoman Empire. Sultan Mahmud who had fiercely announced his intention that 'he would never allow the interference of foreign powers

31

11　Navarino Bay: the destruction of the
Turkish-Egyptian fleet in 1827 upset the
balance in the eastern Mediterranean and raised
the spectre of a Russian attack on Constantinople

in his relationship with his own subjects' would soon have to eat his
words. Already the Anglo-Russian protocol of 1826 had paved the
way and now the representatives of England, Russia, and France
were to meet on the island of Poros to decide the nature of the new
Greece.

Meanwhile, what had become of the Greeks? In 1822, they had
proudly proclaimed in the Constitution of Epidaurus the formation of
a National Assembly. Yet political feuds and rival Assemblies proliferated throughout the war and made a final solution seem no nearer.
It is a tribute to the political skill of Count John Capodistrias, the
first President of Greece, elected in 1827, that negotiations with the
allies were carried on successfully.

The Great Powers had been forced by events to take more notice of the war as it progressed. English policy was influenced by the fear, expressed by Canning, that Russia would 'gobble Greece at one mouthful and Turkey at the next'. After the accession of Tsar Nicholas I in 1825, Russian interest in the Greek question waned but her relations with the Sultan became more strained. The dramatic defeat of the Turkish navy at Navarino Bay persuaded the Tsar to attack the Turks the following year, the one thing Canning had tried to prevent. At the Treaty of Adrianople (1829), the Sultan, with no more cards to play, was forced to accept the mediation of England, France, and Russia.

By that year, the last Turk had left Greece; three years later, the crown of an independent Greece had been offered to Prince Otho, the son of the King of Bavaria. Against all odds, the Greeks had triumphed. 'What is a Greek?' Metternich had scornfully asked at the beginning of the war. By 1832, he had his answer. The success of the Greeks did not pass unnoticed among the other tributary states of the Ottoman Empire. As Toynbee has put it: 'The first explosion of Greek nationalism kindled the first spark of its Turkish counterpart.'

3 Crisis in the Levant: The Revolt of Mehemet Ali

IT IS TEMPTING at first sight to link the nationalist revolts in the Balkans with the Egyptian crisis of the 1830s, and to see the latter as the first move to create an Arab Empire in the Near East. But despite superficial similarities between the two movements, there are also fundamental differences.

Although Egypt was destined later to become the focal point of Arab nationalism, a direct appeal to this in the 1830s would have been meaningless, not least because Mehemet Ali, the leader of the Egyptian revolt against the Porte, was himself an Albanian. This was not the only obstacle to creating a feeling of Arab nationalism; a further difficulty lay in defining what an Arab actually was. Perhaps Metternich might have more appropriately asked: 'What is an Arab?' This is not easy to answer even now and no easier today than it was in the nineteenth century. With the spread of Islam, religion, not the place or origin began to condition the use of the term. It is only within the last half-century that the West has lumped the Arabic-speaking nations together and suggested a common unity, formerly unknown.

Before Napoleon, Egypt was dominated by the Mamluks. The word 'Mamluk', means literally 'owned', and it was first used to describe the superior slaves who were imported by their Arab masters from central Asia, especially from the area round the northern coast of the Black Sea. They were chiefly Turks and gradually they rose in the administration and the army and became the dominant caste in Egypt. However, in 1517, the Mamluk sultanate was subjugated by the Ottoman Turks and in 1639, with the conquest of Iraq from Persia, almost the whole Arab world fell under Ottoman rule. In Egypt, the Ottomans built upon the Mamluk foundations, keeping much of the old order intact albeit beneath the rule of an Ottoman Pasha.

Resentment against Turkish rule found expression in two ways.

12   The massacre of the Mamluks in 1811 at
the hands of the ambitious Mehemet Ali

In the Arab peninsula, there grew up among the Bedouins in the eighteenth century a new puritanical sect called the *Wahhabis*, whose members forbade mystical devotion to holy men and holy places and who accordingly seized Mecca and Medina. In 1818, the *Wahhabis* were defeated by Pasha Mehemet Ali but their beliefs persisted long after they had been officially condemned.

The second focus for resentment occurred in Egypt itself and was centred round the formal opposition of Sufism, organized through Dervish brotherhoods and local craft guilds. Despite sporadic revolts, Turkish oppression was too effective and it was not until the special conditions of the 1830s contrived to bring Egypt into contact with the West that the move towards Egyptian independence was given its impetus.

The history of Egypt for most of the first half of the nineteenth century revolves round the figure of Mehemet Ali. Something of a latter-day enlightened despot, this dark, brooding figure dragged Egypt, however unwillingly, from her primitive ways and forced not only the Porte but also the other powers to sit up and take note.

Born in Albania in 1765, one of seventeen children of the local town watchman, Mehemet Ali first appeared in Egypt as a member of a Turkish contingent sent to help expel the French after Napoleon's return to France. By 1801, he had become one of the two officers commanding Albanian forces in Egypt. Profiting from the anarchic state of Egypt after the French withdrawal, Mehemet Ali ousted his Ottoman and Mamluk rivals for power by a mixture of intrigue and force, and by 1806 the Sultan bowed to the inevitable and invested him as ruler in Egypt. He demonstrated his loyalty by successfully opposing the British, who were forced to evacuate Egypt in 1807. Thereafter he sought to build up his power by ruthlessly exterminating the remaining Albanians and Mamluks in Egypt. The Albanians were destroyed in an ambush in the first *Wahhabi* campaign while the Mamluks were disposed of in the celebrated massacre of March 1811. Walpole's *Travels* contain the reaction of an Englishman to this sombre event:

> Nothing can be imagined more dreadful than the scene of the murder. The Mamluks had left the Divan, and were arrived at one of the narrow passages in their way to the gates of the citadel, when a fire from 2000 Albanians was poured in on them from the tops of the walls, and in all

directions. Unprepared for anything of the sort, and embarrassed for want of room, they were capable of scarcely any resistance; a few almost harmless blows were all they attempted and those who were not killed by the fire were dragged from their horses, stripped naked, with a hankerchief bound round their heads, and another round their waists, they were led before the Pasha and his sons, and by them ordered to immediate execution. Even there the suffering was aggravated, and instead of being instantly beheaded, many were not at first wounded mortally. They were shot in different parts of their bodies with pistols or stuck with daggers.

But if the keynote of Mehemet Ali's rule was arbitrary and brutal oppression, it was not wholly destructive. His reforms had a predictably military bias. His aim was to create a European-type army and, to pay for it, he began to break up the feudal order and improve agriculture and stimulate the lucrative cotton trade with England. Western teachers were imported for his new schools, Western books were translated and printed on the new printing-press set up in Cairo, and students were sent to Europe to imbibe Western culture. As the country became more prosperous, the army was expanded and brought more up to date, principally by European military adventurers, lured by high rates of pay and the rich prizes to be won.

If he was not already aware of it, the failure of the Ottomans to subdue the Greeks must have alerted Mehemet Ali to the weakness of their rule and aroused in him thoughts of further Egyptian expansion. He was irritated too by what he considered to be the base ingratitude of the Sultan in not rewarding him adequately for all he had done for the Ottoman Empire in Arabia and Greece. As early as 1822 he had been given control of operations against the Greeks in Crete and three years later a large Egyptian force under his able and ambitious son, Ibrahim Pasha, landed in the Peloponnese. Something has already been said of Ibrahim's military successes in Greece, although his total lack of naval experience was to prove his undoing at the Bay of Navarino. To look at, he was short, fat, and ugly with a black beard only partly covering the scars of smallpox. But notwithstanding his unprepossessing appearance, he was a brave, if cruel, soldier, and contemporaries ascribed to him great dignity and personal presence. He became the principal instrument of his father's policies as the years went by.

Both Ibrahim and his father decided to cut their losses after the

13   Ibrahim Pasha (1789–1848), the adopted
son of Mehemet Ali

Egyptian evacuation of Greece and, while the Sultan bargained with
the Great Powers over Greece, seeking to stave off the imminent
Russian threat, Mehemet Ali turned his attention again to Syria, a
province he had intended to conquer since 1812. Under pressure, the
Sultan had promised him the three *pashaliks* into which Syria was
then divided, in return for military assistance if the Ottoman Empire
was attacked by either Britain, France, or Russia. Mehemet Ali was
in no mood to help the Sultan any more; in any case, he had his own
personal vendetta to wage against Ibrahim Pasha, the ruler of Syria,
who had harboured refugees from Egypt and whose rich trade in
coal, timber, and silk was well worth the cost of a campaign.

Ibrahim was given command of the Egyptian army and the campaign against Syria, though delayed by a widespread cholera epi-

demic, began towards the end of 1831. Held up during the winter by the sturdy defence of Acre by his namesake, he then began to sweep all before him. Proceeding quickly northwards, he took Damascus in June and summarily defeated Ottoman armies at Homs and Beylan in July. Much to his disgust, he received orders from his father telling him not to press home his advantage against the Ottomans in Anatolia itself. For the next five months Mehemet Ali was to seek in vain confirmation of his conquest of Syria from Sultan Mahmud. The Sultan, who had been slow to respond to this threat from the south, dug his heels in firmly and refused to give way. So Mehemet Ali authorized his armies to advance and at Koniah in the heart of Anatolia on 27 December 1832 the Ottomans were put to flight and their commander, the Grand Vizier, taken prisoner. This was Ibrahim's moment of glory and nothing now stood between him and Constantinople; nothing that is, save for the Great Powers.

Once again the three countries most intimately concerned with this disruption in the Near East were Britain, France, and Russia. Britain's foreign policy under Lord Palmerston, Earl Grey's Foreign Secretary, was directed towards achieving a settlement of the tortuous Greek problem above all else. It was to this end that the British Ambassador at the Porte, Stratford Canning, promised British support for the Ottomans against Mehemet Ali as the price of their acceptance of the Greek settlement. Meanwhile Mehemet Ali was angling for a British alliance himself, although at first with little success. At the time of Ibrahim's successful conquest, the British government, preoccupied with events nearer home, adopted a policy of sitting on the fence – a policy that the Russians were quick to exploit.

The French, traditionally closer than Britain to Egypt, were not able to exert much influence either. Mehemet Ali could count on some French sympathy for his cause, but no active help, even though the French star at Constantinople had been waning somewhat since the days of Napoleon. So the two more liberal powers, Britain and France, were unable to throw much into the balance – unlike Russia, whose interests were more directly concerned with the fate of the Ottoman Empire. Mahmud had virtually no choice but to appeal to Tsar Nicholas for aid. The Tsar had good reasons for intervention besides the customary bias towards southwards expansion.

He had no wish to see a strong Egyptian replace a weak Turk at Constantinople and, if he had no illusions about the weakness of the Ottoman Empire, he wanted to be the only vulture in the sky when the end came. The Sultan delayed his appeal to the Tsar for as long as possible but the advance of the impulsive Ibrahim to within 150 miles of Constantinople forced his hand. In February 1833 he formally invited a Russian army of 30,000 men to cross the Danube and at the same time a Russian squadron sailed into the Bosphorus.

This was a momentous event. The Sultan now felt strong enough to stand up to Mehemet Ali, but not until the troops actually arrived. In the meantime, he granted him the right of governorship of the three Syrian *pashaliks* and allowed Ibrahim the title of *Mohassel* (collector of taxes) in the rich province of Adana. The English and French viewed askance the intervention of Russia but could do little about it beyond urging Mehemet Ali to accept the Ottoman concessions. This he did, and was reconfirmed in his title as Pasha of Egypt.

Much more significant, however, than the temporary resolution of the Ottoman-Egyptian crisis was the signature on 8 July 1833 of the Treaty of Unkiar Skelessi between Russia and the Porte. This was a defensive treaty that was to last for eight years. It confirmed the Treaty of Adrianople and the Greek settlement and it provided for each country to help the other in the event of outside attack. More important was the secret clause stating that the Porte would close the Straits to foreign warships, 'not allowing any foreign vessels of war to enter therein on any pretext whatever'. The Russians were at pains to explain to the other powers that this treaty gave Russia no new rights *vis-à-vis* the Porto but it was difficult to escape the impression that it gave Russia a *de facto* suzerainty over the Ottomans which was utterly repugnant to Britain and France. It is certainly possible to detect a heightening of Russophobia in Britain from this date, which was to have important implications for the future.

The 'Second Mehemet Ali Crisis' occurred simply because Sultan Mahmud was bent upon avenging his humiliation at the hands of the Egyptian Pasha. Reforms were initiated throughout the Ottoman Empire and the army brought more up to date. The Sultan looked in vain for help from Europe but Palmerston, who held no brief for Mehemet Ali, would not support the Sultan either until he appeared to stand a chance of winning. The Russians too were anxious not to

14 The Russians join the Turks at Unkiar Skelessi. The treaty later signed here alarmed the West about Russian intentions towards the Ottoman Empire

upset the *status quo* in the Near East now that they had what they wanted. It was Mehemet Ali, now an old man and anxious to resolve the crisis, who provoked one by declaring himself in May 1838 to be independent of the Sultan. Palmerston persuaded him to withdraw the statement but it was apparent that the Pasha had by no means given up the idea. Anyway, the Sultan forced the issue into the open by declaring war on Mehemet Ali in April 1839.

Once again the weakness of the Ottoman army was exposed. At Nezib in northern Syria, Ibrahim defeated the Ottoman force. Mahmud II died before this disastrous news reached him, although he would have been still more stunned by the defection of the Ottoman fleet to the Egyptians a week later. Constantinople was in a state of panic. The new Sultan, Abdul Mejid (1839–61), a mere boy of sixteen, offered Mehemet Ali hereditary possession of Egypt but Mehemet Ali demanded Syria and Adana too. Such concessions would have quite removed the fiction of Ottoman unity and at this moment the five major powers stepped in to save the Sultan's face. They invited the Porte to suspend any final determination without

41

their concurrence, thereby taking over the responsibility of coercing Mehemet Ali to accept a settlement. He refused their terms at first but the bombardment of Beirût and Acre helped him to make up his mind. He was granted 'the Government of Egypt together with the additional privilege of hereditary male succession'. His army was still limited and he was subject to Ottoman laws and taxes. This legal relationship was to last for some seventy years.

Egypt had been cut down to size. Certainly her resources were insufficient to bear the burden of administering Syria, and her subsequent history would not suggest that her earlier ambitions were justified. Mehemet Ali continued to pursue dreams of further dominion by stirring up revolt in the Lebanon in 1841 but his influence was now negligible. The ogre of the 1830s was a forgotten man when he died in 1849, just eight months after the death of his son Ibrahim.

15   The bombardment of Acre (November 1840) by Admiral Napier, Second in Command of the British Mediterranean Fleet. This cut Ibrahim's communications and forced him to evacuate Syria

4 The Era of Reform

ON 3 NOVEMBER 1839, Sultan Abdul Mejid issued from the imperial palace at Ghulane a decree named the *Hatt-i Serif*, more commonly known as the *Tanzimat*. It was an attempt by new institutions to obtain the benefits of a good administration for the provinces comprising the Ottoman Empire. The reforms listed included security of life and property, the establishment of a penal code, a regular method of taxation, and a system of military recruitment to include Christian as well as Muslim subjects of the Porte. Although this decree directed attention to the empire's effort to reform itself from within, it was only one of a series of reforms that date from the accession of Sultan Mahmud II in 1808 and which continued at intervals until 1871.

Why did Sultan Mahmud consider reform necessary, and what was the nature of the empire which he and his successor tried to reform? It is probable that Mahmud's mother was the celebrated Aimée Dubucq de Rivery, a beautiful Creole who had been captured by Algerian Corsairs and sent as a gift to Sultan Abdul Hamid I. It was she who influenced with her Frankish ways his nephew Selim, the initiator of reform in the nineteenth century. Upon his death in 1807 and the accession of Mahmud she became the Valideh Sultan, or mother of the Sultan, a position of great importance. Although schooled in the traditional Turkish way, Sultan Mahmud had not been kept in the strict seclusion of his forbears, and had no doubt been influenced by his mother. He preferred to sit on a chair not a divan. He drank champagne in open defiance of Muslim law. He hired Signor Donizetti, the brother of the famous composer, to teach him the skills of Western music. Strict Muslims looked aghast at the Sultan's encouragement of the study of anatomy, for did not the Koran state that 'even if the dead man had swallowed the most precious pearl, and that pearl not his', the opening of the body was forbidden? When Sultan Mahmud ventured out disguised into his

16   Aimée Dubucq de Rivery, the beautiful
Creole captured by Algerian corsairs and
presented to Sultan Abdul Hamid

capital he did not have to go far to hear tales of incessant Janissary
atrocities. It is easy to see why the Sultan conceived his loathing for
those twin bastions of reaction the Church and the Janissaries.

What of the state that the Sultan hoped to reform? It is exceedingly
hard to generalize about Turkey in the first half of the nineteenth
century. The Turk himself had certain characteristics of which
changelessness was the essence. Historically nomadic, the Osmanlis
remained thus, a feature reflected in the lack of permanence in the way
they decorated and arranged their dwellings. To the true Turk,
agriculture and military service were the only honourable occu-
pations; commerce and trade should be left to the infidel races.
Extraordinarily uninterested in widening his knowledge, the Turk
was profoundly lazy in an Oriental sense. Bliss to him – known as
kerf – was to recline in the shade, smoking and listening to the sooth-

44

ing murmur of running water. Much of this apathy stemmed from the fatalism of the Muslim faith. With admirable qualities of courage, self-discipline, and hospitality, the Turks were essentially international parasites. They conquered and took what they wanted, leaving behind them no trace of an indigenous culture or civilization. A Turk would happily pull down a Greek temple if he wanted the stones.

It is possible to deride the successive attempts at reform as being still-born and little more than window-dressing for the benefit of the Great Powers who alone seemed capable of saving the empire from the consequences of the revolt against its rule. It must be admitted too that as relations between Britain and Russia deteriorated, Palmerston and others demanded evidence of Turkish reforms before offering the Sultan help. Also, the most feverish period of reform coincided with the most serious threats to Ottoman security and when the danger subsided so too did the reforms. This, however, may be explained by the contrast between the two reforming Sultans: Mahmud II was energetic and innovative; his successor Abdul Mejid was not. More revealing perhaps is the concern expressed by the Russians, who of course had a vested interest in Turkey remaining a lifeless corpse, at the surprising success of her reforms.

It has been suggested that it was unwise to try and Westernize the Ottoman Empire; that by showing insufficient respect for long-cherished Islamic customs, Mahmud damaged irrevocably the secure base upon which a more modern state could be built. Another view was advanced by a contemporary, von Moltke, a young Prussian lieutenant, later the famous Field-Marshal, who wrote:

> For the accomplishment of his purpose it was indispensable for him to raze to the ground any other authority within the compass of the Empire and to unite the whole plentitude of power in his own hand; to clear the site before setting up his own building. The first part of his great task the Sultan carried through with perspicacity and resolution; in the second he failed.

The charge has further been brought, however, that in attempting to Westernize the empire, the reforming Sultans either did not do it fast enough or that in doing it at all they gave birth to a new generation of reformers who were to accelerate its break-up. It is difficult to see

45

what other course Sultan Mahmud could have followed. Like Peter the Great in Russia, a century before, he was aware that the need for an efficient army was imperative. Threatened by the Greeks and then the Egyptians, the Sultan did not have the time to consider the sensibilities of his subjects. His was the stark choice between change or collapse. Later reformers may well have bungled the application of their reforms and the forces of reaction may have set in momentarily after 1871, but the course had been firmly set. It was above all from the schools and academies established by Mahmud and his successor that there emerged a new intellectual élite, more widely travelled and steeped in Western mores than their forbears. For them there could be no going back.

Sultan Mahmud was twenty-three at the time of his accession. At first he was involved with the war against Russia, and after the Treaty of Bucharest in 1812 he concentrated on depriving the local Pashas in Rumelia and Anatolia of the considerable degree of autonomy that they enjoyed. Clearly the Sultan was not content to be a mere *primus inter pares*. But as the need for improvements in the army manifested itself, the clash with the Janissaries became inevitable and in 1826 Mahmud addressed himself to this task. Already before him, he had the example of the Egyptians, fellow Muslims, whose army had been modernized and whose superior fighting qualities had been revealed in the Greek campaign. No longer could this proud corps of Janissaries be allowed to hold the empire to ransom by their entrenched opposition to new methods and equipment.

The Sultan chose his moment well. In 1826, at the height of the Greek campaign, he resurrected the *Nizam-i Cedid* of Selim III, but to satisfy the Chief Mufti and the senior Janissary officers, he maintained that he was merely restoring the military order of Süleyman the Magnificent. The Janissaries viewed it differently. On 15 June they overturned their soup-kettles in their traditional gesture of revolt, ready to repeat the massacre of 1807. This time the Sultan could rely on loyal officers to defend him and the Janissaries were no match for their heavy cannon. The Corps was ruthlessly exterminated and formally abolished. The 'Auspicious Incident', as it came to be called, removed finally the principal barrier to the enforcement of the Sultan's personal rule.

Now a more modern army was needed. The office of *Serasker* was established, combining the functions of Commander-in-Chief, Minister of War, and Chief of Police. A force of 12,000 to serve for twelve years was to be raised in Constantinople. It was one thing to raise the men; it was quite another to train them. Mehemet Ali was unlikely to help, while Britain and France were regarded as too sympathetic towards Greek insurgents. It was largely through the contact with von Moltke, who visited Constantinople in 1835, that an important link was established with Prussia, and officers were subsequently sent from there to help in the military academies. The German-Turkish link, so significant in later years, had been forged.

A constant hazard facing the German and other European military advisers was the savage scorn with which the Turkish soldiers regarded their Christian mentors. Mere technical proficiency might be respected by the Turk, but it would never alter his belief in the inherent superiority of the Muslims over the infidel. It was only the more educated who could restrain their prejudices. As von Moltke observed

The Colonels gave us precedence, the officers were still tolerably polite, but the ordinary man would not present arms to us, and the women and children from time to time followed us with their curses.

The logical corollary to military reform was reform of the local and central administration. Here the Sultan had to tread more carefully. He was free to act only within the provisions of the *Sharia* and was far from being the autocrat that many Western observers claimed. The whole structure of government was based on a nice balance of separate interests that ranged from the Chief Mufti, the Ulema, the Beylerbeyi or military feudal commanders in Rumelia, to the Patriarchs of the Millets, the officers of the Dervishes and guilds down to each separate village with its headman. To superimpose a more centralized system required a mixture of tact and ruthlessness. The Janissaries no longer existed to give vent to popular resistance to change by military force, but a lack of co-operation among government officials could just as effectively vitiate proposed changes. A common grievance was their insecurity of tenure and the suddenness with which their posts might be confiscated. So Mahmud issued in

1826 a *Hatt-i Serif*, which closed the Court of Confiscations, renounced the reversionary rights of the Treasury to heirless property, and took away the power of life and death from the Pashas. The loss of revenue was more than made up by the new-found confidence and efficiency of the civil servants – an increasingly important class in Ottoman society. In 1831, the Sultan, anxious to conscript further men for his army and to rationalize taxation, conducted the first modern census of the male population in Anatolia and Rumelia. More radical still was the attack on feudalism in the same year, through the abolition of the *timars*. These were military fiefs, previously granted to *Sipahis* or cavalrymen in exchange for military service. Although by the nineteenth century most of them had been converted into crown lands and then leased out to tax-farmers, many still remained. The *Sipahis* were either pensioned off or absorbed into the cavalry of the Sultan's army. The *timars*, approximately 2,500 in Anatolia and Rumelia, became part of the crown domains.

Sultan Mahmud placed the organs of central government under his critical scrutiny too. Here he was less successful for he was too much influenced by the effect he hoped to make on the West. The introduction of frock-coats, desks, and all the paraphernalia of Western bureaucracy did not significantly affect the realities of government or the administration of justice. Any changes could be brought about only after reducing the independence of the Ulema. In 1826 the position of the Chief Mufti was reduced by the transference of his office to that of the former Aga of the Janissaries. No longer could he issue arbitrary rulings on matters of education and justice; now his office was more of a government department and therefore more directly beneath the control of the Sultan. Later on control of education passed to a separate Ministry of Education and legal administration came under a Ministry of Justice. A further limitation of the Chief Mufti's power was the gradual assumption of control by the Sultan of the pious foundations, the *Evkâf*. These were originally grants of freehold land for pious purpose, not unlike the chantries of pre-Reformation England. They were administered by *Mütevelli*, men who were often members of the Ulema. Thus a large amount of formerly freehold land had fallen over the years under the aegis of the Chief Mufti and his lieutenants. Mahmud's establishment of a

17　A traditional school in Anatolia. Sultan
Mahmud II, 'the Reformer', recognized the need
for encouraging primary and secondary education

separate Ministry of *Evkâf* sought to divert any surplus, after the
administrative costs had been paid, into the state treasury. Even the
Sublime Porte itself was not able to escape unchanged. Ministries of
Civil and Foreign Affairs were set up and in 1838 the title of Grand
Vizier, although restored later, was replaced by that of Prime
Minister and committees for trade, agriculture, industry, and public
works were set up.

So far it will be seen that Mahmud concentrated primarily on
attacking those institutions which blocked the path to reform. But,
like Mehmet Ali, he was no mere destroyer. His actions served as the
catalyst by means of which the Ottoman Empire came to transform
itself. Nowhere were these changes more important than in the field
of education. Here Mahmud made his principal contribution and,
while some of his other measures of reform may be dismissed as
transitory, these may not. The Sultan wanted trained officers and
civil servants. For this more schools were required and the language
barrier had to be overcome. At first, he concentrated on schools with a

military bias. The naval and military schools, founded in 1773 and 1793, were revived and encouraged. In 1827, a medical school was opened in Constantinople followed by an Imperial Musical School in 1831 and a School of Military Sciences in 1834. More revolutionary were the two grammar schools (*rusdiye* schools) which he set up for here was a great departure from tradition in recognizing the importance of primary and secondary education. The Sultan began to tackle the problem of language by active encouragement of Turkish students travelling abroad. For example, in 1827 four students were sent to Paris, despite strong opposition to the proposal. Soon this trickle would become a flood. Few of the nationalist reformers later on in the century were to be unfamiliar with Europe.

None of the Sultan's reforms would have succeeded but for his personal example. He departed from the age-old tradition of cutting himself off from the labours of state and regularly attended the *Divan*. He also set about reorganizing the Imperial Household, mercilessly suppressing all titles without duties. In matters of dress, he turned from the reforms of the military to reform of civilian dress as well. He decreed that the fez, which ironically originated from the Greeks, should replace all other forms of headgear; and that robes and slippers should give way to cloaks and black leather boots. In all of this, and it should be remembered that dress was closely connected with religious status, the Sultan himself pointed the way. It is probably true, however, that the sailor Adolphus Slade was echoing the feeling of the majority of Turks when he wrote:

In no one thing did Sultan Mahmud make a greater mistake than in changing the mode of mounting the Turkish Cavalry, which before had perfect seats, with perfect command over their horses, and only required a little order to transform the best irregular horse in the world into the best regular horse. But Mahmud, in all his changes, took the mask for the man, the rind for the fruit – European cavalry rode flat saddles with long stirrups; therefore he thought it necessary that his cavalry should be the same.

Even though the ruling of the Holy Law of Islam on vital matters such as marriage, property, and the status of women was still unaffected and unchallenged by the changes Mahmud had wrought, it is hard to deny the importance of what he started.

When Abdul Mejid became the Sultan in 1839, the stage was

18 The Imam was the upholder
of the sacred law of Islam

already set. Behind the Sultan there lurked his formidable mother Valideh Sultan Bem-i Alem who had little difficulty in controlling her sixteen-year-old son. The new Grand Vizier was Husrev Pasha but the chief architect of reform was to be the new Foreign Minister, Reshid Pasha. The reformers had already begun the work of preparing the *Tanzimat* – the Reorganization – and, undismayed by the imminent threat from Mehemet Ali and his war-like son, they pressed on to complete it by the end of the year.

The *Tanzimat* itself contained many bold statements of intent but none more radical than the demand for equality before the law for people of all religions. This struck at the heart of Ottoman society for it involved a renunciation by Muslims of the theory that the Christians who lived within the empire were their inferiors. While they were considered as such, the Muslims were prepared to grant them a large measure of toleration, notably through the Millet system. But to

19   Lord Stratford de Redcliffe, who did much to
reinforce Turkish resistance to Russian ambitions

admit the Christians to equality of status was unthinkable. The long
and painful history of religious toleration in western Europe, and the
history of the Negro in the United States, show the extent of what the
Sultan was asking his people to accept. The *Tanzimat* must have given
further offence by its insistence on 'new rules'. The Prophet Mohammed is supposed to have said: 'The worst things are those that are
novelties, every novelty is an innovation, every innovation is an error,
and every error leads to Hell-fire'. The reference to 'new institutions'
in the Noble Rescript was hardly consistent with this.

It was principally in the law that the *Tanzimat* broke new ground.
In 1840, a new Imperial Rescript laid down the lines for the reorganization of the Council of Justice and in May 1840 a new penal
code was drawn up. The latter was muddled and ineffective at first,
but it involved a significant move away from the Holy Law. At first
the significance of this seems to have escaped the Ulema, but when
Reshid Pasha tried to introduce a new court of justice to hear com-

mercial disputes, he was promptly dismissed. This was a savage blow to the reform movement for he was the driving force behind many of the proposed changes and his ambitious plans for a new system for the administration and taxation of the provinces was still-born.

Even so, the reform movement became active again after 1845 and with Reshid Pasha back at the Ministry of Foreign Affairs, the Sultan issued a new rescript, the *Hatt-i Humayun* in which he complained about the ignorance of the population and the need to concentrate on civilian life now that the military changes were completed. To translate his words into action he summoned an Assembly of Provincial Notables to try and discover what else needed to be done. Having learnt little, he resorted to roving commissioners in the provinces, who discovered very little more. However, more attention was given to education and more secondary schools were built, though by 1850 there were only six of them with 870 pupils. The decision to start building the first Ottoman State University was taken but the building was abandoned when the walls were only a few feet high. Reshid Pasha went calmly on and in 1850 managed to secure the acceptance of the Commercial Code for which he had been dismissed in 1841. But soon the reactionaries were clamouring again for his blood and, with his dismissal from the Grand Vizierate in 1852, the first period of reform ended. In 1851, Lord Stratford de Redcliffe (as Stratford Canning now was), the British Ambassador to the Porte, wrote: 'The great game of improvement is altogether up for the present.'

The pressures of the Crimean War, the blatant inadequacy of institutions and offices set up bravely in the name of democracy but which needed more time to be given a fair trial, the fierce opposition of the Muslim dignitaries and those whose positions and prestige were put in jeopardy by the reforms, and the ever constant shortage of money – the Turkish piastre fell from 23 to £1 sterling in 1814 to 104 in 1839 – all these factors worked against the reformers. Credit perhaps should go to both the reforming Sultans, particularly Mahmud, who grimly continued to try and save their empire from a premature grab by the Tsar or from a further revolt from within. There was a certain heroic defiance in their belated attempts to save their heritage.

5 The Threat from Russia: War in the Crimea

THE DECADE OF REFORM from 1840 saw the Ottoman Empire relatively free from outside interference. The rock upon which this period of peace was founded was the Straits Convention of 13 July 1841. This formal agreement signed by Britain, Russia, Austria, Prussia, and France endorsed the Sultan's intention to maintain 'the ancient rule of the Ottoman Empire' by which foreign warships were forbidden to enter the Straits while the Porte was at peace. Controversial though this provision became later on, the treaty underlined the withdrawal of Russia from her privileged position opposite the Ottoman Empire. For the time being she presented no immediate threat to Turkey – a state of affairs that would not last long.

While Sultan Abdul Mejid devoted himself to the pursuit of reform, he could not afford to ignore the threats to his control in the outlying provinces of the empire. These were but the prelude to the subsequent clash with Russia in the Crimea, but they proved a constant drain on Ottoman resources and encouraged the Russians to think that the days of the empire were numbered. One of the basic errors Tsar Nicholas made was in underestimating the Ottoman will to resist.

The first problem facing the young Sultan, once Mehemet Ali had been forced by the Great Powers to withdraw his claims to Syria, concerned the Lebanon. Here the biblical Mountain of the Cedars was by tradition a feudal principality under the suzerainty of the Sultan. Ibrahim's Syrian campaign had left the Lebanon in a state of anarchy. It was the intention of the Sultan to reduce it to the level of an ordinary provincial governorship. In 1840 a puppet ruler, Beshû-el Kassim was duly replaced by Omar Pasha, one of those curiously ubiquitous figures who occasionally rose to prominence in the Ottoman state. A Croat by birth, he had originally tutored the Sultan in calligraphy, but then joined the army and fought against Ibrahim at the Battle of Nezib. His position as Provincial Governor was of short duration, for France objected on behalf of the Maronites, and the Sultan was forced to accept a dual system of government, in which the Mountain was divided into two administrative districts, one for the Druses and one for the Maronites. The Turkish authorities ordered all Europeans to leave the Mountain, an order which prompted an ultimatum from the French Ambassador to the Porte demanding redress of numerous grievances. The appearance of a French frigate off Beirût persuaded the Turks to yield and the next decade saw peace once again in the Lebanon.

Further north in the Principalities there were signs of incipient nationalism crudely kept in check by the Tsar. Moldavia and Wallachia were both governed in accordance with the *règlement organique*, a decree drawn up under Russian auspices in the 1830s. In this the Russians had set up a strict oligarchy in which the cultivators of the soil were exploited ruthlessly by the nobles, a class the Russians assiduously supported. However, under the enlightened rule of George Bibescu in Wallachia and Michael Sturdza in Moldavia, ambitious programmes of reform to improve the lot of the peasants were undertaken. Discontented nobles turned to the Russian Consul for help at a time when Michael Kogalniceanu and others, who had studied abroad and learned of the past glories of the Roumanian race, were returning from Europe, armed with the reforming programme of the 1848 intellectuals. This included the demand for constitutional reforms and the creation of parliamentary democracy as well as placing great emphasis on personal liberty.

The revolution in Moldavia broke out on 8 April 1848 but was quickly put down by Sturdza, who could not afford to alienate his Russian masters. More serious was the uprising in Wallachia where Bibescu was forced to annul the *règlement organique* and then fled the country. A party of moderates, anxious not to touch the suzerain rights of the Sultan, gained power and promptly attacked the rights of the nobles. The Tsar cunningly suggested that the Ottomans should interfere and support the *status quo*. A clash between Ottoman troops and Wallachians gave the Russians an excuse to invade the Principalities once again. By the Convention of Balta Liman, 1 May 1849, Russia and the Porte re-established order and the revolution was dead.

Suppressed though it was, the Roumanian revolution stirred up public opinion and the Roumanians elicited considerable sympathy from British and French observers. The Tsar was seen more and more as a reactionary figure and public opinion in Britain mounted against him. More important, British statesmen had begun to realize that the forces of Balkan nationalism could be used as a bulwark against Russian aggression towards Constantinople.

Serbia was another Balkan country whose struggle for independence from the Porte necessarily involved the Great Powers in her domestic politics. During the 1830s Milosh ruled as an autocrat. In 1835 a conspiracy against him led to the drawing up of the democratic Constitution of Sretenje which was suppressed in the face of opposition from Austria, Russia, and the Ottoman Empire. Meanwhile Palmerston, alive to the possibilities of intervention, sent Colonel Hedges in 1837 as the first British Consul to Serbia. His aim was to urge the Sultan to enforce a more liberal régime and in this he was partly successful. A Senate of seventeen life members was set up and disputes with the Prince were to be referred to the Sultan. Milosh was not the man to accept such a restriction of his powers; but his attempted resistance resulted in his enforced abdication in June 1839. He was followed as Prince by his two sons, first Milan and then Michael, but the progressive policy of the latter alienated the conservative Serbian peasantry. In 1842 Michael was forced to cross the Save, the traditional gesture of abdication, and a National Assembly elected in his place Alexander Karageorgevich, the last surviving son of Karageorge, the hero of the War of Independence. Tsar Nicholas objected to his election; Lord Aberdeen, now the British Foreign Secretary, supported it. With concessions on both sides, Alexander remained as ruler. The effect of the revolution of 1848 was to bind Serbia more closely to Austria, whom she supported against the Magyars. Conversely, a number of Austrian Serbs entered the service of Alexander and the feeling of a common Serbian heritage was enhanced. The Sultan could only view with misgivings this anti-Ottoman drift.

The Serbs in Bosnia caused him still further trouble. They had resisted Sultan Mahmud's reforms initiated through the Ottoman Governor and had risen under the 'Dragon of Bosnia', Hussein-Aga, one of the most romantic figures in Bosnian history. Together with Mustafa Pasha, another Bosnian *kapetan* he preached a Holy War against the Sultan and denounced the reforms of Mahmud. For a time Hussein-Aga and Mustafa overran most of the northern plain of Anatolia but their victory was short-lived. Hussein-Aga was defeated on the fatal plain of Kossovo where four and a half centuries before Bosnian Christians had fought in vain against the Ottomans. The Bosnian reactionaries predictably opposed the *Tanzimat* decree of Abdul Mejid who accordingly sent his trusted Omar Pasha to crush the resistance. With Bosnia and Herzogovina under his control, Omar Pasha settled down in Sarajevo, the new seat of government, and ruled as Governor-General for nearly twenty years. But the mutual animosity of Christian for Muslim was never far beneath the surface.

South of Bosnia lay the little Adriatic state of Montenegro. A branch of the Serbian family, these men of the mountains were independent of the Sultan and governed by Prince-Bishops, the succession passing from uncle to nephew. Her proximity to Austria caused Montenegro to glance nervously northwards and inevitably the Sultan became implicated in her fate. In 1851, Peter II, the last ruler of the Black Mountain, died. He was succeeded by his nephew, Danilo, who was determined to change the theocratic form of government. Young, and in love with a beautiful girl from Trieste, the restrictions attendant upon his position held little appeal for him. Thus in 1852 Montenegro was declared an hereditary temporal principality. The Tsar and the Hapsburg Emperor approved; Sultan Abdul Mejid did not. Five separate Ottoman forces attacked the little state, at which the Austrians intervened on Montenegro's behalf. The peace of 3 March 1853 by which the Sultan was constrained to accept the *status quo* served only to emphasize his failing prestige in the extremities of his empire.

The problems of a multi-national empire set against the backcloth of mounting national feeling left the Sultan once again a pawn in the hands of the Great Powers. None of them wanted war. But as so often happens, a misinterpretation of motives, abetted by bungled diplomacy, resulted in warlike postures, from which there was no retreat. Tsar Nicholas believed that by his personal intervention the British could be kept quiet. He bargained without the British public. The remote autocrat was incapable of gauging the extent of Russophobia that had built up in Britain towards the end of the 1840s. In

20 The heads of Montenegrin 'rebels' are
brought before the Pasha. Their country did
not achieve independence for another thirty years

France, Louis Napoleon, desperately casting round for popular
support, was unlikely to throw up the chance of standing firm behind
the Sultan. Tsar Nicholas, meanwhile, certain of the Ottoman
Empire's imminent collapse, devoted his attention to schemes for
partitioning it when the time came. There was no need to go to war.
A show of force in one of the numerous weak-spots of the Ottoman
Empire would be enough, so he thought, to achieve his ends. The
Austrians had forestalled him in Montenegro where he had hoped to
pose as the special protector of the Orthodox Church and to make an
Ottoman refusal to make peace with Montenegro a *casus belli*. It was
not long before he could once more use religion to foster a quarrel
that would eventually lead to the summoning of fleets and armies.

For many years, Catholic and Orthodox monks had quarrelled
over the rights of their respective Churches in Jerusalem, Bethlehem,
and Nazareth. In 1740, new Capitulations had been signed between
France and the Porte in which it was declared that the French
religious Orders should not be disturbed in their occupation of the

church of the Holy Sepulchre at Jerusalem. This and other important privileges reflected the superior position of the 'eldest daughter of the Church' at that time. Since then, however, the Greek Orthodox had attracted many more pilgrims to the Holy Land and their followers were demonstrably more pious than the Latins. During the 1840s Russia and France began to take up supporting positions behind their respective groups. Personal antipathy entered into it too. Tsar Nicholas looked upon Louis Napoleon as a parvenu and addressed him as 'my dear friend' instead of using the customary phrase of monarchs, 'my brother'. For his part, Louis Napoleon hoped to expunge from his people's memory his exile in London and his assumption of the Imperial title by scoring a diplomatic triumph over the Tsar. The Sultan found himself in the uneasy position of having to adjudicate between the two factions; he made the mistake of trying to please both. In a note of 9 February 1852 he directed that the keys of the great church at Bethlehem must be given to the Latins 'as of old'. By a separate *Firman* he reaffirmed the custom of giving the keys of these sanctuaries to the Greeks, Latins, and Armenians and said that 'no change' should be made in the present state of the gates of the church of Bethlehem. The Ottomans took refuge in diplomacy but in December 1852 under French pressure they handed over the keys to the Latins. The Tsar was furious and now adopted a new tack.

The British had no particular interest in the fate of the Holy Places. It was, however, the erroneous belief of the Tsar that he could trade on Anglo-French tension to enlist British support. He placed great faith in the somewhat meaningless agreement he had reached with Peel and Aberdeen in 1844 in London, and when Aberdeen formed his coalition government in 1852 the Tsar believed he could rely on him. It was upon this assumption that Tsar Nicholas outlined his plans for the ultimate disposal of the Ottoman Empire in his celebrated conversations with Sir George Hamilton Seymour, the British Ambassador to St Peterburg in January 1853. The Tsar suggested that none of the Great Powers should have Constantinople but that the Principalities should come under Russian protection. Britain would be compensated with Egypt and Crete. It is unlikely that he was considering active intervention but he just wanted assurances of British support if, as he thought likely, the Ottoman Empire collapsed.

We have on our hands, a sick man – a very sick man; it will be, I tell you frankly, a great misfortune if one of these days he should slip away from us.

It was through subsequent correspondence between the Tsar and Russell, the new British Foreign Secretary, that the suspicion grew in London that the Tsar might take matters into his own hands and try and precipitate the fall. The British could certainly not accept this.

Meanwhile the Tsar was embarking on an even more dangerous course of action. In February 1853, he sent to Constantinople as his special envoy Prince Menshikov, a soldier not a diplomat. His brief, outlined by Count Nesselrode, the Russian Foreign Minister, was to re-establish Orthodox privileges in the Holy Places and to ensure that the granting of the key to the great church at Bethlehem left the position there unaltered. Menshikov went out of his way to insult his hosts. He committed a gross breach of etiquette by appearing for his first audience in civilian dress, not in uniform. He refused to treat with Fuad Pasha, the Ottoman Foreign Minister, who was replaced by Rifaat Pasha. Stung by such treatment, the Ottomans employed their traditional delaying tactics. They may have taken comfort too at the thought of British and French backing. Even more reassuring for them was the return on 5 April of Lord Stratford de Redcliffe, 'the voice of England in the East'. How much he influenced the Ottoman resolve to stand up to the Russians will remain a matter for debate. In any case, on 5 May, Menshikov suddenly demanded within five days an agreement guaranteeing the position of all Orthodox Christians within the Ottoman Empire. This was a revolutionary demand. It went far beyond any previous Russian request and was tantamount to saying that they demanded the right to interfere on behalf of two-fifths of the total population of the Ottoman Empire. Such a thinly veiled exercise in political intervention was too much for the Ottomans. On 10 May they refused to accept the Russian proposals; on 27 May diplomatic relations between the Porte and St Petersburg were broken off.

War could not now be averted. The Tsar, believing wrongly that he could carry the Austrians along with him, continued to bring pressure on the Ottomans and in July occupied the Principalities. With a French fleet off Salamis and a British squadron outside the Dardanelles, the situation in June 1853 looked ominous. Last-minute attempts

21 The Church of the Holy Sepulchre at Jerusalem. It was French insistence in 1842 that they should be allowed to help repair this church which led to mounting friction between Catholic France and Orthodox Russia

to lessen the tension were made. Count Buol, the Austrian Foreign Minister, convened in Vienna a meeting of representatives from Britain, France, and Prussia. The result was the Vienna Note, proposing that the Sultan respect the rights of the Orthodox Church, that all privileges enjoyed by other Christian sects should be extended to the Orthodox Church, and that no change in the existing position of his Christian subjects should be made without reference to France and Russia. On 20 August 1853 the Ottoman Grand Council, incensed at not being consulted, rejected the Vienna Note. They were clearly in no mood to be dictated to and Stratford de Redcliffe may well have encouraged them to stand firm. By now demonstrations in Constantinople advocating war with Russia revealed the bellicose mood of the Turkish people. Despite a last-minute attempt by Count Buol to revive the Vienna Note, the situation had gone too far for retreat. On 29 September the Sultan ratified the decision of the Grand Council for war with Russia. On 30 November an Ottoman squadron was annihilated by the Russians at Sinope –

a legitimate act of war but hysterically regarded by the British as an act of treachery. On 4 January 1854 the British and French fleets sailed into the Black Sea and, following a defensive treaty with the Porte, the two governments declared war on Russia on 28 March 1854.

The war itself was to prove as aimless and confused as the events leading up to it. Ironically, the Ottomans, whose interests perhaps were most closely involved, found themselves offered up as cannon-fodder for the Russian guns, thanks largely to British and French military incompetence. At first, all went well for the allies. The Austrians, sensitive to the presence of Russian forces in the Principalities, were anxious to see them go. The failure of the Russians to capture the fortresses of Silistria, defended by some young British officers and a gallant force of Turks, sparked off their retreat northwards. Count Buol scored a notable diplomatic triumph by urging the Tsar to evacuate the Principalities. Frederick William IV, King of Prussia, urged the Tsar to concur and on 2 August the last Russian soldier crossed the river Pruth and the Principalities were occupied by an Austrian garrison. It is possible that the war might have ended there. The Tsar, however, was unlikely to forgive the Austrians and at a conference in Paris the anti-Russian allies agreed on the Four Points, thereafter to be their war aims. These were the abolition of the Russian protectorate of the Danubian provinces, the free navigation of the Danube, the complete introduction of Turkey into 'the European equilibrium', and finally the renunciation by Russia of her exclusive patronage of the Balkan Christians.

Now that a campaign on the western borders of the Black Sea was precluded, the British cast round for an alternative theatre of operations and fastened on the Crimean port of Sebastopol. The British public settled back happily, regarding the whole affair as an exercise in martial sport, while the French clung to their customary illusion that war means glory. On 1 September 1854, the English and French forces landed on the Crimean peninsula and under their respective commanders, Lord Raglan and Marshal Saint-Arnaud, began the march to Sebastopol. On 20 September they arrived at the stream of Alma where they were confronted by the Russians, commanded by Menshikov, more at home on the battlefield than in the audience chambers of diplomats. Chiefly through the dash of the French

22 'Into the valley of death rode the six
hundred.' Lord Cardigan's celebrated but
disastrous cavalry charge against the Russian
guns at Balaclava

zouaves, the Russians were decisively defeated. Unhappily this dash
was not sustained and the chance to follow up the Russian retreat and
take hold of Sebastopol was lost. Two days later the march was
resumed but by then it was too late.

The story of the calamitous siege is well known; for a year it was
the pivot round which the fate of the war revolved. Basing his decision
on inadequate intelligence, Raglan resolved to march round to the
south of the town, giving Todleben, in charge of the Russian defences,
time to throw up some barricades. On his way, Raglan suddenly
encountered Menshikov who was just returning from having given
orders to scuttle the Russian Black Sea fleet in the mouth of the harbour.
After risking this surprise defeat, Raglan settled down to lay siege to
the town but although the British and the French possessed unques-
tionable military superiority, they were unable to breach Todleben's
defences or to prevent Russian reinforcements and supplies filtering
to the city from the north. Furthermore, the British fleet was im-
peded by the sunken Russian ships from coming close enough to the
city, while Menshikov kept on harassing the besiegers. He scored

one success on 25 October by capturing the redoubts at Balaclava, famous for the charge of the Light Brigade, later immortalized by Tennyson. The comment from General Bosquet: 'C'est magnifique, mais ce n'est pas la guerre', could well have applied to much of the campaign.

At Inkerman on 5 November Menshikov was less successful and again in the following August he was driven off by a mainly French force. By then, however, the demands of the Russian winter and the ravages of cholera had taken their toll of the British and French armies. A conference to discuss the Four Points was summoned at Vienna. Before it met, Tsar Nicholas died, having just heard that the despised Turks had repulsed his troops at the harbour of Eupatoria on 17 February. The new Tsar, Alexander II, refused to countenance any reduction of the Black Sea fleet and the bombardment of Sebastopol continued. At last on 9 September 1855, Sebastopol fell. The war dragged on for a little, and the Russians captured the fortress of Kars in Asia Minor from the Turks, but the new Tsar was anxious for peace and so were the allies. On 25 February a congress of the Great Powers met in Paris and hostilities ceased.

Thanks largely to the Great Powers, the Russian thrust southwards had again been parried. The Ottomans would now enjoy a short respite from their northern neighbour's attacks; and the time might even have been used to put their own house in order while there was still a chance. Two factors made this impossible. In 1861 Abdul Mejid died and was succeeded by the incompetent and reactionary Sultan Abdul Aziz (1861–76). Secondly, the rise of Panslavism weakened still further the already shaky Ottoman rule in the Balkans.

6 From Paris to Berlin: Ottoman Decline Divides Europe

THE PEACE OF PARIS marked a watershed in the attitudes of the Great Powers towards the problems of the Near East. The treaty itself left the map, with one exception – the cession by the Tsar of the southern part of Bessarabia to Moldavia – exactly as it had stood before the war. The Powers were anxious to admit the Porte into the 'comity of nations', and to try and bolster her up for the last time by a mixture of enforced reform from within coupled with legal safeguards to protect her frontiers – particularly from Russia.

As it transpired, neither of these aims was to play so important a part in achieving a period of comparative peace in the Near East for the next twenty years as the preoccupation of the Powers with new problems of their own. There was no mistaking the harshness of the Black Sea clauses nor the intention of the Powers to turn Russian eyes away from Constantinople. Henceforward, the Tsar would have to march behind the banner of Panslavism in the Balkans if he wished to extend Russian influence southwards. Although the English and the French had fought side by side in the Crimea, Napoleon III had come to regard the Ottoman Empire as immune to reform and Anglo-French interests in the Near East were beginning to conflict. Besides, Napoleon's ambitions towards Italy, shortly to be involved in the Risorgimento, disposed him towards building up an alliance with Russia. In Britain, there was a growing feeling that the preservation of the Ottoman Empire was a lost cause and as the prospect of a canal through the Isthmus of Suez began to take concrete form, the strategic value of Constantinople as the key to the overland route to India came to seem less essential. It was Disraeli who made the mistake of thinking that the Ottoman Empire could alone act as an effective obstacle to Russian aggression: the nearly independent and vital states of the Balkans would have been a much safer horse to back. The two German states of Prussia and Austria were less concerned with the fate of the Ottoman Empire. Prussia, so soon to

MAP NO. 3
The Ottoman Empire in Europe 1856

dominate western Europe, was anxious only to protect her status as a
Great Power. Austria, however, was more closely involved and her
ill-fated attempt to replace Russia as the protectress of the Principalities was to result in Roumanian independence, not an extension
of Hapsburg power.

66

Few of the clauses of the Paris treaty would survive the test of time but they offer a pointer to the direction events in the Balkans were beginning to take. The principal clause, already mentioned, was the guaranteeing of the 'independence and integrity of the empire'. No European Power could declare war on the Sultan without first seeking the mediation of a third Power. The Sultan was to provide for the welfare of his Christian subjects by implementing the *Hatt-i Humayun*. Possibly the most important clause was the neutralization of the Black Sea; it was to be open to all merchantmen and closed to all warships. The Russians understandably would spend the next fifteen years trying to change this clause. Thirdly, the Principalities were no longer to be a Russian protectorate. Instead they were to have an 'independent and national administration', under Turkish suzerainty and the guarantee of the Powers. A European commission was to 'meet without delay at Bucharest', to propose 'the bases of their future organization'. Here lay the germ of the principal dispute in the Near East for the next ten years.

The increasing nationalist feeling in the Principalities had been exacerbated by the Crimean War, and it became apparent that the only safeguard against the perpetual incursions of foreign troops was independence. Already Bibescu had removed the fiscal barrier between the two Principalities; by 1847 Roumanians in Paris were arguing that each state should have the same ruler. Napoleon III was in favour of a measure of unity; Austria and the Porte were hostile to the idea. Britain was lukewarm – Lord Clarendon, the Foreign Secretary, referring to Moldavia as 'a little barbarous province at the end of Europe'. After considerable negotiating between the Great Powers in 1857–8, the Roumanians took the matter into their own hands. At the elections in Moldavia, Separatists and Unionists were still wrangling when a Colonel Couza was put forward by a Unionist, Jassy Pisoki, who put his back against the door with a pistol in his hand and threatened to shoot himself if his colleagues did not make up their minds before leaving the room. In the circumstances, they agreed and Couza was elected Prince on 17 January 1859. Amidst scenes of disorder he was then chosen by the *Divan* in Bucharest as Prince of Wallachia. Fortunately for Roumania the war between Austria and France monopolized the attention of the Powers and on 31 May the Porte reluctantly agreed to recognize Alexander Couza

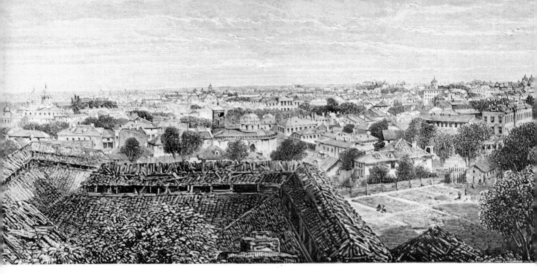

23 The old city of Bucharest, capital of Wallachia. The onion-shaped Orthodox church domes remind one of Russian claims to spiritual protection over the Principalities

as the ruler of both states. There was still some way to go to full independence but the obstacles were thrown up by the Principalities themselves, not the Great Powers.

The now familiar process of disintegration was continuing elsewhere in the empire. The Porte, with its resources overstretched, could indulge only in delaying actions to stem the tide. There was little hope that the Sultan would do anything. Abdul Mejid was the last Sultan to die before he was deposed. Conspicuous for his lack of distinction, he ruled at a time when the frail foundations laid by Mahmud urgently needed to be built upon. Instead, Abdul Mejid chose to wallow in extravagance and luxury and for over twenty vital years the power to dictate events slipped from the Sultan's grasp. When he died in 1861 at the age of thirty-nine, the doctor attributed his death to consumption; in reality he died because of his gluttony and sexual excesses. His harem abounded with literally hundreds of beautiful odalisques, drawn from all corners of his empire, although not a single woman could be Turkish in case she might consider herself in any way equal to the Sultan, the One, the Unique. At meals, the Sultan, having consumed whole legs of mutton and drowsy with the scent of carnations, cinnamon, and coffee would fall asleep at the table, at which all would turn their heads away, for

no unprivileged eye might contemplate his slumbering majesty. Leading such a life, his support of the reforming programme was a token one, to put it mildly. When he died, foreign loans had reached a total of £180 million while four-fifths of the money originally designed for the 'regeneration of Turkey' had been appropriated by the Sultan for his personal use. While it had taken nine years to build a single iron bridge in Constantinople, the Sultan had given his architect, the Armenian Balian, absolute freedom of expenditure to build the Palace of Dolma Bagtche with its Corinthian columns and French frescoes, its huge table of malachite and lapis lazuli, and the largest plate-glass mirror ever made. Small wonder that the Great Powers began to regard the Ottoman Empire as beyond redemption while the tributary states, fired by new nationalist creeds, sought to break the links with the past.

The final years of the reign of Sultan Abdul Mejid were darkened by the news of further clashes in the Lebanon between the Druses and the Maronites. Once again, scenes of butchery occurred at sites familiar to Christendom from the Bible. The British Consul reported that 5,500 Christians perished in Damascus. The French used the incident to suggest a French occupation of Syria – in the end they sent half of a European force of 12,000 – although Napoleon III was probably only bringing pressure to bear on the Sultan to make him give up his opposition to the French proposal to build a canal at Suez. The British, alarmed at their designs in the East, managed to

24　The Cretan revolt (1866–9) was supported
by Greece but, as the Great Powers showed
little interest, the Turks suppressed it with
comparative ease

secure the French evacuation from Syria and in 1861 the Sultan
agreed to the Charter setting up the autonomous Lebanon under a
Governor-General, to be a non-Lebanese Christian. Despite endemic agrarian problems, the settlement in the Lebanon was the most
successful example of autonomy applied to a Turkish province.

The Cretan insurrection could not be solved so simply. Habitually
ungovernable, these islanders complained about their fiscal burdens
and the unpopular Governor-General, Ismail Pasha, and demanded
various reforms from the new Sultan. By 1866, with little hope of
securing their reforms, the Cretans began to demand union with
Greece. A wave of anti-Turkish feeling in Athens encouraged the
rebels who, in September 1866, declared Ottoman rule abolished and
proclaimed union with Greece. The Cretans fought fiercely against
Mustapha Pasha who lost two-thirds of his army in the first year of
the revolt. Yet, not for the first time, the Turks were able to make a
little capital out of the divided aims of the Powers. The record of

70

independent Greece had not been an impressive one, and the Powers were reluctant to see Crete come under the rule of so unstable a state. Neither the British nor the Russians were ready to contemplate the total disintegration of the Ottoman Empire. Confident therefore of some support, the Sultan imposed on Crete 'The Organic Statute of 1868' which granted her a measure of autonomy, though not her cherished plan for union with Greece. The Greeks continued to send volunteers to Crete to stir up revolt among the islanders until 11 December 1868 when the Porte sent them an ultimatum. By now the Great Powers were heartily sick of the whole affair and under the aegis of Napoleon III and Bismarck a conference met at Paris and persuaded the Greeks to desist. The Sultan had scored a partial victory.

Storm-clouds were now gathering over the Balkans. In Serbia, Alexander Karageorgevich had been deposed and replaced by the original founder of Serbia, Milosh Obrenovich, now seventy-nine years old. In 1860, Milosh died and was followed by Michael Obrenovich III, possibly the greatest ruler Serbia has produced. His principal aim was to obtain the withdrawal of the Turkish garrisons from the fortresses in Serbia, a constant source of friction between Serbia and the Porte. Clashes between Turks and Serbs in Belgrade led to a conference of the Powers at Constantinople where, under Austrian pressure, the Sultan agreed to abandon the Turkish quarter of Belgrade. By 1867 the Turks had evacuated the two remaining fortresses in Serbia.

Prince Michael's most spectacular achievement was the embryonic union of the Balkan peoples against Turkish rule which, save for his untimely assassination in 1868, might have changed the course of Balkan history. His pattern of alliances started in 1866 with a treaty with Montenegro, whose army had achieved a dramatic victory over the Turks at Grahovo (1858). In 1867 another treaty followed, this time with the Greeks, which provided for the annexation of Bosnia-Herzogovina by the Serbs as a *quid pro quo* for the cession of Epirus and Thessaly to the Greeks. Finally, in 1868, Prince Michael made a separate treaty with Prince Charles of Roumania. Had Prince Michael availed himself of a chance offered in 1866 by Austria's involvement in war with Prussia, he could have launched a powerful army against the Sultan. Still, the opportunity was lost and after

1867 Austria, who had no wish to see nominal Turkish control removed from the Balkans, was able to bring Serbia once more under her thrall.

The Eastern Crisis of 1875–8, resolved finally by the Congress of Berlin, virtually removed Turkish influence from Europe. It was not brought about solely through the incessant irruptions against Ottoman rule. Serious though these were, it is possible that the Porte could have held on a little longer in preserving the last vestiges of an empire in Europe. This would have been possible only without the appearance of the movement known as 'Panslavism'. Disunited though the Balkan people proverbially were, they became sufficiently imbued with this ideal to rise up together and raise the alarm among the Great Powers. Tsar Alexander II was able to use it as a powerful weapon of propaganda, a veil to cover the age-old ambitions of Russia towards Constantinople.

Panslavism originated first in Austria-Hungary. 'Scattered Slavs let us be one united whole and no longer be mere fragments', wrote Jan Kollár, a Slovak, in 1824. The first ethnic and linguistic conference was held at Prague in 1848 and the Russian troops sent by Tsar Nicholas to fight against the Magyars were regarded as fellow Slavs working towards a Panslavist goal. In Russia, the movement began only gradually. The first University Chair of Slavonic Studies was set up in 1811 but to begin with Slavophils thought in terms of religion not race as the unifying factor. Professor Pogodin emphasized the unity among a great federation of Slavonic peoples and this feeling gathered strength in Russia after the Crimean War. It was not yet an important popular movement but it provided for Ignatiev, the fiery and aggressive Russian Minister in Constantinople, a justification for the extension of Russian hegemony southwards and for nullifying the Black Sea clauses of the Peace of Paris. It was likely then that if the ambitions of Ignatiev were to prevail over the more sober counsel of the cautious Russian Foreign Minister Gorchakov another conflagration in the Balkans would offer Tsar Alexander the opportunity to draw attention away from the widening cracks in his government at home by scoring military successes abroad. This time Bulgaria was to open the gate through which the Tsar could enter the Balkan imbroglio.

Panslavism came comparatively late to Bulgaria. It was principally through Russian encouragement after the Crimean War that Bulgarians, profiting ironically from their education in the new Ottoman schools, began to see the possibilities of a nationalist movement. Ideas from Russia flowed in, notably through the merchant colony at Odessa, but to begin with their feelings were not violently anti-Turkish. The Bulgars, like other Christian subjects of the Sultan, had been encouraged to play their part in the administration of the empire and they would probably have settled for an autonomous state under the Sultan. The key issue was religion. The stranglehold maintained by the Greek Orthodox Church led to strained relations between Bulgars and Greeks in which the Russians supported the Bulgarian side. The Porte, therefore, by a *Firman* of 13 March 1870, created a Bulgarian exarchate which recognized the Slavs as a separate religious nation, independent of the Greek Patriarch at Constantinople. The Sultan knew what he was doing for disputes and bitterness between the different Christian factions proliferated in the early 1870s. To the awakening of Slav feeling in Bulgaria was added the bland announcement by the Russians in 1870 that they were no longer bound by the Black Sea clause of the Treaty of Paris. Not only this, but the Porte was seething with discontent, the twin result of financial stringency and the revolutionary movement of the Young Ottomans. In such an electric situation, it was merely a matter of time before the Sultan would have to mobilize the Turkish army in defence of his empire.

The Eastern Crisis began in an obscure village in Herzogovina. Two incidents prevented it from remaining merely 'an internal affair of Turkey'. The Turks had slaughtered a band of Montenegrins in 1874 at Podgoritza, causing the Tsar to protest, for he regarded himself as the natural champion of the Orthodox Serbs. The Austrian Emperor had visited the Dalmatian coast in 1875, thus giving the Catholic clergy cause to look to Austria for aid. It was this clash of interests between Austria and Russia that lay behind the extension of the conflict. Austria regarded Bosnia-Herzogovina as being effectively within her domain and thus opposed the Russian suggestion of local autonomy for the two states beneath the Porte. Russia, on the other hand, regarded herself as the upholder of Slavic interests in the Balkans. The Sultan was in his usual role of having to accept what the Great Powers decreed. Andrassy, the Austrian

25   Batak, a village in Bulgaria being sacked by
the Turks in 1876. The Bulgarian Massacres
did much to prompt anti-Turkish feeling in
Britain

Foreign Minister, put forward the first peace proposals in a note of
1875. The Sultan reluctantly agreed to his suggestion that he should
grant religious liberty, land reforms, and the abolition of tax-farming
in the two states. After the pro-Russian Montenegrins had sprung to
the help of Bosnia-Herzogovina, Andrassy was forced to make
further concessions in the Berlin Memorandum of May 1876. The
Sultan, supported by Disraeli, was infuriated by the high-handed
way in which Andrassy threatened to enforce the new settlement, if it
was not implemented.

Meanwhile in Bulgaria, a fresh revolution had broken out with the
connivance of Serbia, and the Turkish authorities put it down with
unexampled severity. It is thought that over 12,000 Bulgarian
Christians were slaughtered in May 1876. The Bulgarian atrocities
revolted the Western world and Gladstone's pamphlet *The Bulgarian*

Horrors and the Question of the East did much to turn public opinion against the Ottomans. 'Let the Turks', he wrote, 'now carry away their abuses in the only possible manner, namely by carrying off themselves, their zabtiehs, and their mudirs, their bimbashis and their yuzbashis, their kaimakams and their pashas, one and all, bag and baggage, shall, I hope, clear out from their province they have desolated and profaned.' In this mood, Britain was unlikely to leap to the defence of the Sultan against Russia. In July, Serbia and Montenegro declared war against the Porte on behalf of their brother Serbs.

Chaos now reigned in Constantinople. The year 1876 became known as the 'year of the three Sultans' and again events in Constantinople suggested that there was little hope of firm leadership to cope with the mounting crisis. Abdul Aziz had proved no better than his predecessor. Except for a visit to Paris, he had never left his capital. The new telegraph system brought news to him of peasants in Anatolia and Armenia being obliged to sell their children in order to buy flour to keep themselves from starvation. He was unable to grasp the complexities of the revolts in the Balkans or the conflicts between Christian and Muslim. Rather than grapple with what was beyond him, the Sultan indulged in his favourite game of chasing cocks and hens over the royal apartments and when they became entangled in the hangings, he placed the highest orders about their necks, recalling for himself the great days of Turkish history. Eventually, the burden of taxation and the record of failure led to the Sultan's deposition. He was succeeded by the Crown Prince Murad but three days later the deposed Sultan was discovered dead with his wrists slashed. The new Sultan Murad V's mind was possibly so unhinged by this news that by the end of August he had agreed to make way for the succession of his scheming half-brother Abdul Hamid (1876–1909). This harsh unbending man was to initiate the so-called 'Hamidian tyranny'. In attempting to turn the clock back and rejecting innovations from the West, he would bring nearer that cataclysm from which the new Turkey would emerge.

It was now essential for Austria and Russia to reach an agreement. In July 1876 an agreement was drawn up at Reichstadt, but the Tsar was unable to check the Panslavic movement he had unleashed. The Panslavic Cherniaev was commanding the Serbian army while money for the beleaguered Serbs poured in from Russian banks.

26 Sultan Abdul Aziz
whose repressive rule
inspired the Young
Ottomans

27 Sultan Murad V,
deposed in favour of
Abdul Hamid II in 1876

The collapse of the Serbian army before a more numerous Turkish
force led the Tsar to concentrate his attention on Bulgaria. At this
stage, the attitude of the Powers was all-important and it was out of
their divisions that the war between Russia and the Ottoman Empire
was created. Bismarck, who saw a partition of the Ottoman Empire
as the best means of resolving the quarrel between his two fellow
members of the Dreikaiserbund, was anxious to achieve a settlement.
However, anti-Turkish feeling was growing in Russia and the Tsar
was more and more faced with the prospect of 'war or disorder at
home'. Lord Derby suggested a gathering of the Great Powers at
Constantinople to which the Sultan agreed as the only alternative to
war with Russia. Bulgaria remained the chief problem. The Sultan,
profiting so he thought from the differences of the Powers over the
fate of Bulgaria, calmly announced that his empire was now reformed
and he could mend his own fences without foreign help. With
deliberate perversity the Turkish officials affected not even to know
what the word 'Bulgaria' meant; for them it was a mere geographical
term for the region north of the Balkans. With Austria bought off

28 San Stefano, where peace terms between
Russia and Turkey were signed in 1878, a
preliminary to the more conclusive Treaty of Berlin

by the promise of Bosnia-Herzogovina, Russia declared war on the
Porte on 24 April 1877.

The Russian advance was slow and came to a halt at the fortress of
Plevna in Bulgaria. Under the inspired leadership of Osman Pasha,
the Turks held the Russians off until December when the fortress
fell. The British viewed with alarm the southern advance of the
Russians over the Balkan mountains. By 28 January, Adrianople had
fallen to the Russian General Skobelev, while another army had
conquered Armenia. The British fleet was ordered up to Constantinople on 23 January but the order was countermanded and they did
not leave until 9 February. In any case, the British were unable to
prevent the Turks from suing for peace and accepting harsh Russian
terms on 31 January 1878. It was one thing for Russia to make peace
with the Porte; it was quite another to satisfy the British.

The Peace of San Stefano was signed between the Russians and the
Turks on 3 March. The Russian demands were moderate but not
moderate enough. She agreed to evacuate Erzerum in Armenia but
demanded southern Bessarabia from Roumania. Bosnia-Herzogovina she was bound to leave to Austria but in so doing alienated the
Serbs who were granted Nish but not Bosnia, which they dreamed of

77

annexing. Again, Bulgaria was the difficulty. By insisting on a new, enlarged, and independent Bulgaria which would command the approaches to Salonika and Constantinople, the Russians were asking for the impossible. In fact the Tsar, like his opponents, misread the situation, for Bulgaria was unwilling to substitute for the effective suzerainty of the Porte that of St Petersburg. Still, the fear was there and Britain and Austria-Hungary demanded a European congress for revising the terms of San Stefano. Before the Powers met at Berlin, Lord Salisbury, the new British Foreign Secretary, persuaded the Russians to reduce their demands in Bulgaria while Disraeli agreed with the Sultan that if Russia annexed Armenia, the British would occupy Cyprus 'the key of Western Asia'.

The Congress of Berlin which met on 13 June established on paper at least a settlement for the Balkans that lasted for thirty-four years. This was the last example of diplomacy in the grand style. Everything was arranged to suit the interests of the Great Powers; the lesser Powers, whose future was being decided, were not even represented. Twenty-two out of the fifty-four articles of the final treaty dealt with Bulgaria; but no Bulgarian could vote on the outcome. Lord Beaconsfield, as Disraeli now was, wrote to Queen Victoria on 17 June: 'All questions are publicly introduced and then privately settled.' The Russians tried to renege on their promise to the British about Bulgaria, but in the end big Bulgaria was trisected along the previously agreed lines. Bosnia-Herzogovina was to be 'occupied and administered' by Austria-Hungary. The Austrians were to occupy militarily the corridor between the two Serbian states of Serbia itself and Montenegro – the Sanjak of Novibazar. Russia gained Bessarabia from Roumania but had to recompense her with two-thirds of the Dobrudja. Serbia, Montenegro, and Roumania were all declared independent states. In Asia Minor, Russia secured Ardahan, Kars, and Batum – the acquisition of the last of these causing a flurry among the British who feared Russian encroachment round the Black Sea. In reply, Beaconsfield broke the news of the Anglo-Turkish Cyprus Convention of 4 June by which Britain planned to occupy Cyprus in order to guard against any further Russian attacks against Ottoman territory. The Sultan Abdul Hamid promised 'to introduce the necessary reforms in the provinces inhabited by the Armenians'.

Such were the provisions of the new charter. The need for real

MAP NO. 4
The Balkans at the Treaty of Berlin 1878

independence in the Balkans had been recognized although the
acquisition of Bosnia-Herzogovina by the Hapsburgs would create
Austro-Serb rivalry in the future. Beaconsfield's Asiatic policy of
checking Russia by bolstering up the Ottoman Empire with the promise of British military support was soon to be exposed as hopelessly
outdated. Feeling in Russia was that having won the war, they had

lost the peace; and for this they blamed the British. Perhaps the most significant change of all was the signature between Andrassy and Bismarck of the Dual Alliance in October 1879. The ground was being prepared for the division of Europe into two hostile camps to be resolved only by the Great War (1914–18). It is unlikely that such a coalition would have been created but for the events of the Eastern Crisis of 1875–8.

29   A sketch of Lord Beaconsfield (Disraeli) walking wearily through the streets of Berlin to attend a session of the Congress of Berlin

7 Young Ottomans and Young Turks: 1856-1914

THE SECOND HALF of the nineteenth century witnessed dramatic changes in the movement to reform the Ottoman Empire. The Imperial Rescript (*Hatt-i Humayun*) of 18 February 1856 translated into more concrete terms those measures of the *Tanzimat* decree which sought to give full equality to all Ottoman subjects.

> Let it be done as herein set forth. All the Privileges and Spiritual Immunities granted by my ancestors . . . to all Christian communities . . . shall be confirmed and maintained.
>
> No subject of my empire shall be hindered in the exercise of the Religion that he professes.
>
> The organization of the Police . . . shall be revised.
>
> The most prompt and energetic means for remedying the abuses in collecting the Taxes and especially the Tithes, shall be considered. The system of direct collection shall gradually, and as soon as possible, be substituted for the plan of farming, in all branches of the Revenues of the State.
>
> Steps shall be taken for the formation of Banks.
>
> Steps shall also be taken for the formation of roads and canals.

This was certainly a grandiose plan for reform but without the personal lead of the Sultan the statement amounted to little. However, the conservative leadership of Ali Pasha and Fuad Pasha did encourage the young intellectuals to improve their knowledge of French while the Great Powers kept a paternal eye on Turkish efforts to reform. In the new Ottoman lycée at Galatasaray, Muslims and Christians sat side by side discussing with comparative freedom the ideas of the day. Cevdet Pasha's *Mecelle*, the new legal code completed by 1876, was to remain in force until 1926. Even under the corrupt rule of Sultan Abdul Aziz (1861–76) and the harsh reign of Sultan Abdul Hamid (1876–1909) – in many ways a time of reaction and repression – much was achieved in the fields of education, the law, and communications.

Two important trends can be detected which were to alter the course of reform radically and divert it into stormier channels. The first of these was the resentment of the younger Ottomans, drawn from wide social and ethnic backgrounds and educated in the improving Ottoman schools, against the growing autocracy of the Sultan and his Ministers. Now that the traditional checks, such as the janissaries, against an authoritarian Sultan had been removed, he could act with much greater impunity against what he considered the dangerously liberal ideas of the young reformers: and if, as was the case with Abdul Aziz and Abdul Hamid, the Sultans were personally reactionary, they could become an impregnable barrier against change. The thought that the Sultan's power should be restricted, if not capable of political expression, was expressed in the 'Ode to Reshid Pasha' written in 1856 by Ibrahim Sinas:

Your law is an act of manumission for me,
Your law informs the Sultan of his limits.

It would not be long before other writers were demanding a constitutional government primarily as a check to the personal authority of the Sultan and his Ministers.

The second change that was taking place was even more important. This centred round a debate over whether the adoption of the apparatus of Western civilization was correct in the first place. There were those who saw the Western Powers as leeches sucking away the life-blood of Islam. They could point among other things to the growing dependence of the Turkish government on foreign loans to shore up the newly created Ottoman Bank (1861). Since the Balkan states were beginning to see the benefit in Panslavism as an ideal, why should the Sultan not embrace the Panislamic creed? Sultan Abdul Hamid was astute enough to see the possibilities of this and was to follow a policy of deliberately cultivating the Muslims throughout his empire. That he failed was largely due to the presence of the Christians in his dominions. He could massacre the Armenians, but this was hardly the final answer. Later on in the days of the Young Turks, the battle would be fought between those who wished to see a decentralized empire and those who thought in terms of Turkish domination. In the final analysis, the revolutionaries were not so concerned with the religious differences as the need to preserve the Turkish State. The disasters of the Great War were to force them to follow the only practicable ideal – Turkish nationalism (*Yeni Turan*).

But this was all far in the future. Turkish nationalism was comparatively slow to develop but it received its first impetus from a group of young revolutionaries known as the 'Young Ottomans'. Theirs was the first hesitant step towards some degree of constitutional government, although they were united only in condemning what they saw as the arbitrary rule of the Sultan and restrictive ideas of his elderly reforming Ministers, Ali and Fuad Pashas. The Young Ottomans were influenced by writers such as Ziya Pasha and Namik Kemal. Namik Kemal had travelled widely in Europe and was particularly impressed by London which he called 'the embodiment in stone of the indomitable power of public opinion against authority'. How different this was from Lenin's vituperative blast some thirty years later against what he regarded as the bastion of plutocracy! In common with other Muslim intellectuals, Namik Kemal saw no inconsistency in trying to adapt the constitutional ideas contained in Montesquieu's *Esprit des Lois*, which he read avidly, to the principles of the *Sharia*. He observed that,

Every book treats the subject of political rights with different subdivisions. However, the points on which the greatest measure of agreement exists among authors are such general principles as the sovereignty of the nation, the separation of the powers, the responsibility of officials, personal freedom, equality, freedom of thought, freedom of the press, freedom of association, enjoyment of property, sanctity of the home.

To keep the government within the limits of justice, there are two basic devices. The first of them is that the fundamental rules by which it operates should no longer be implicit or tacit, but should be published to the world . . . The second principle is consultation, whereby the legislative power is taken away from the government.

Here was no root and branch rejection of the old but an intelligent attempt to graft new and strange ideas on to an established system of law. Above all he wanted to see free institutions and an educated body of public opinion.

The Young Ottomans began their protest with the Kuleli incident in 1859. A few conspirators planned to assassinate Sultan Abdul Mejid but the plot was discovered and the leaders dispatched to

83

Asia. The movement gathered strength in the 1860s and the first organized group, numbering Namik Kemal among its members, met in 1865. The *eminence grise* behind the revolutionary movement was none other than the son of Ibrahim Pasha of Egypt, Prince Mustafa Fazil. He based himself in Paris from where he criticized the Sultan's régime and where he was joined by Young Ottomans fleeing from the retributive measures of Ali Pasha. In 1868, this group produced their first paper, *Hürriyet* (Freedom), to which Kemal contributed articles. Before long, however, splits occurred in the ranks of the Young Ottomans. In 1867, the Sultan Abdul Aziz made a state visit to France and Mustafa Fazil used the opportunity to ingratiate himself with his ruler. He was duly rewarded by being brought back to Constantinople where he eventually became a Minister at the Porte. The death of Ali Pasha in 1871 raised the hopes of the *émigré* Young Ottomans who returned home full of criticism of the régime. Kemal's play *Fatherland or Silistria* burned with patriotic Ottoman sentiment but brought frowns from the authorities. The government was in any case harassed on all sides. The Sultan had borrowed recklessly to pay for his 'ironclad warships' in the Black Sea and discontent was rife throughout his empire. He possessed neither the wit nor the inclination to cope with the crisis and in May 1876 events overtook him when there was a riot of theological students outside the Sublime Porte. The Sultan was forced to accept a change of government in which Midhat Pasha became the President of the Council of State. Midhat Pasha will always be remembered for his introduction of the Constitution of 1876. Although himself not a member of the Young Ottoman group, he was sympathetic to their ideas, and came nearer to realizing them than any of their number. He was a first-class administrator and had been outstandingly successful as Governor of Baghdad. He had been appointed Grand Vizier in 1872 but disagreements with Abdul Aziz had led to his dismissal after only two and a half months. When Abdul Aziz was deposed in 1876, Midhat Pasha pinned his hopes on the well-intentioned but unbalanced Murad V, whose younger brother, Abdul Hamid, succeeded him on the condition that he accepted the new Constitution drawn up by Midhat Pasha. Cynical and ill-disposed towards reform, the new Sultan lost no time in undermining the plans of the reformers. On 5 February 1877 he secured the dismissal of Midhat Pasha on the grounds of his

30 Sultan Abdul Hamid II.
His long and tyrannical rule came
at a crucial time in Turkish history

being 'dangerous to the security of the state'. To satisfy the Great
Powers the Sultan was bound to accept the Constitution and the first
Ottoman Parliament met in 1877. Comprising a Senate of twenty-
five nominated officials and a Chamber of 120 elected officials, this
new body was unequal to the unprecedented occasion. The speeches
revealed the need for reform but the procedure was irregular. Sir
Edwin Pears reported in the *Daily News* that

> Dr Washburn, the President of Robert College, was present when a
> white-turbanned deputy, who was making a long and prosy statement,
> was suddenly stopped by a stentorian shout from the President of, 'Shut
> up, you donkey.' The orator sat down as if he was shot.

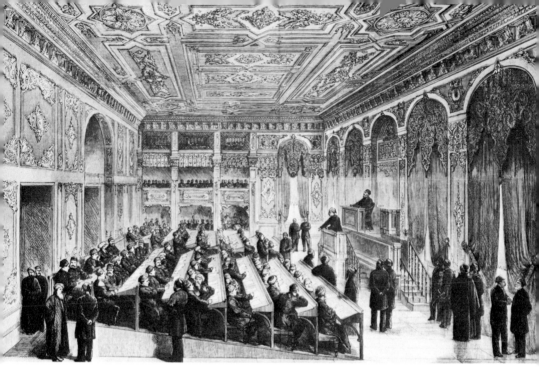

31 The first Ottoman parliament meets in Constantinople
in 1877. This gesture towards democracy was
quickly nipped in the bud by Sultan Abdul Hamid

This Parliament had two sessions but was then summarily dismissed
by the new Sultan, who used the outbreak of war with Russia as a
pretext for its dissolution. No further Parliament met in Constantinople for thirty years; and so ended the dreams of the Young
Ottomans.

Abdul Hamid was a tyrannical autocrat; but his tyranny and
methods of repression served only to strengthen the will of those
whose chief aim was the survival of the Ottoman State. Once again
the Sultan, although he took a more active interest in affairs of state
than his two predecessors, grew into an eccentric of hideous pro-
portions. He was to base what policy he had on the supremacy of the
Turk and the solidarity of Islam. Yet he was convinced that he was
under constant risk of assassination and he surrounded himself in the
Yildiz Kiosk by the most elaborate secret service even by Turkish
standards. The Sultan was armed at all times and was known to
shoot at officials and gardeners at whim. The British Embassy was
once asked to discontinue singing that provocative anthem 'Onward

Christian Soldiers', while the importation of foreign literature was rigidly censored. The Sultan responded to attempts to restore the Constitution with rigid police surveillance of the reformers' activities. A coup to restore Sultan Murad led by Ali Suavi in August 1878 led to Suavi's execution. Ziya Pasha was sent away to be Governor of Adana where he died a bitter man in 1881. Namik Kemal was imprisoned as a common criminal in Constantinople and eventually died on the island of Chicos in 1888.

Where there had once been hope, disillusionment set in. The Sultan surrounded himself with sycophantic admirers. He did his best to muzzle the Press and for thirty years views critical of the régime could only be expressed outside the Ottoman Empire. No one was allowed to mention the name of the deposed Sultan Murad V; and since regicide was a sensitive subject, Turkish news reporters attributed the simultaneous deaths of the King and Queen of Serbia in 1903 to indigestion. The finances of the Ottoman Empire, though stabilized under Abdul Hamid, caused further resentment for opening the door to foreign control. After the declaration of bankruptcy in 1875, the Sultan laid down arrangements with bond-holders' groups for reducing the foreign debt to £106 million. A Council of Administration of the Ottoman Public Debt, mostly composed of foreigners, saw to it that revenues and taxes were collected on behalf of the bond-holders. To the new generation of Ottomans, economic dependence on the Great Powers must have seemed as irksome as political subjection.

Sultan Abdul Hamid's reign, however, was not wholly without its redeeming features. Even he could not abandon entirely the movement towards reform that had been set in motion before his time. The continuation of reform owed much to one of his Grand Viziers, Mehmed Said Pasha (1838–1914), whose lengthy memorandum delivered to the Sultan in 1880 underlined the importance of education and also the need for more 'uprightness' to counter the endemic corruption of state officials. Under his aegis, the programme for building schools gathered momentum. The school for training civil servants (*mülkiye*), founded in 1859 was reorganized and expanded. In 1875 elementary schools (*rusdiye*) were begun, while eventually in 1900 the University of Istanbul came into being.

In order to strengthen his control over the empire, Sultan Abdul

Hamid concentrated on improving communications, particularly railways and the telegraph system. The 1880s saw an enormous increase in railway construction. In 1888 the first railway between Vienna and Constantinople was opened. To pander to Panislamic interests, the Sultan then built the Hejaz Railway between Damascus and Medina. If there was a certain illogicality in the Kaiser William II's visit to Jerusalem as a modern crusader, the outcome of it was the Baghdad Railway project and the strengthening of Turkish-German ties. But even the Sultan's constructive achievements were resented by his people and in the very schools he had created young men and their teachers openly discussed the proscribed writings of their heroes, Namik Kemal and Ziya Pasha.

It was here that the Young Turk movement was born. In 1889 some students from the Imperial Military Medical School formed themselves into a secret society called the 'Committee of Union and Progress'. They took as their blue-print the Italian Carbonari, with their organization of revolutionary cells, and they planned to overthrow the Sultan. Their early history and aims were not unlike those of their predecessors, the Young Ottomans; their achievements were to be more spectacular. An early plot in 1896 to depose the Sultan failed, but although the Sultan shipped off seventy-eight prisoners to military prisons in Tripoli, the movement continued to grow under the ruthless but able leadership of Ahmed Riza (1859–1930) whose headquarters were in Paris. A former member of the 1877 Parliament, Ahmed Riza started in Paris a newspaper, *Meshveret* (Constitution), copies of which were soon finding their way illegally into Constantinople.

Broadly, the aim of the Young Turks was the equality of all Ottoman subjects, the rejection of foreign intervention, and the Ottomanization of the empire. But they were unable to escape the characteristic divisions and feuds of *émigré* politics. First, Murad Bey became leader of the Geneva branch of the Committee of Union and Progress and opposed some of the ideas of Ahmed Riza. When he was persuaded to return to Constantinople where he became, rather incongruously, a member of the Council of State, two young Ottoman princes arrived in Paris and challenged Ahmed Riza's leadership. The most prominent of these, Prince Sabah al-Din (1877–1948) clashed with Ahmed Riza at the first Congress of the Ottoman Liberals held in Paris in February 1902. The Prince, who had set up in Paris a 'League for Private Initiative and Decentralized Branches all over the Asiatic Empire' spoke with the voice of Ottoman liberalism; on the other hand, Ahmed Riza had moved further over in the direction of Turkish nationalism. The two programmes were quite irreconcilable.

While the *émigré* groups wrangled in Paris, the army began to play an important part in the revolutionary movement. Young officers, trained in the Ottoman military academies, began to be excited by the new ideas and would bring an element of ruthlessness into the proposed *coup d'état*. There was in the early 1900s much to excite them. Not only did they find intolerable the scorn with which their empire was held by other nations, but when King Edward VII and Tsar Nicholas II met at Reval to discuss further reforms in the Ottoman Empire their patience was exhausted and they mutinied.

The chief centre of unrest in the army was among the officers of the Third Army Corps stationed at Salonika. Among them in 1906 was a young officer called Mustafa Kemal. Already as a young man he seems to have had that singleness of purpose and drive that was to prove so distinctive later on in his life. While serving in Damascus he had started a revolutionary cell called the 'Fatherland and Freedom Society' and when he was transferred to Salonika, his birthplace, in 1907, he presided over the merging of the different societies into a single Committee of Union and Progress with its headquarters in Salonika.

More important than Mustafa Kemal at this stage was the real leader of the Salonika officers, Enver Bey. When Abdul Hamid ordered an investigation of the Third Army Corps in 1908, Enver Bey and another officer prominent in the councils of the Young Turks, Major Ahmed Niyazi, took to the hills. Semsi Pasha, the general sent by the Sultan to suppress this mutiny, was shot dead in broad daylight. By now the unrest in the Third Army Corps had spread to the Second Army Corps at Edizine. Faced by so serious a revolt and with the Committee of Union and Progress coming out into the open with a demand for the Constitution, the Sultan took refuge in threats and bribery. Such expedients no longer worked. The only course open to him was to give in to the rebel demands. On 23 July 1908, Sultan Abdul Hamid announced that the Constitution was restored.

32   Kamil Pasha, Grand Vizier and elder statesman
of the Liberals, whose policy of Ottomanization had to give way before the exigencies of war

The euphoria of the moment was not destined to last. In a mutual
display of enthusiasm, Armenians and Muslims could embrace each
other in the street; but the problems of ruling this kaleidoscopic
empire remained. It is tempting to attribute to the members of the
Committee of Union and Progress elaborate schemes for constitutional reform. In reality the leaders of the revolt were hard-headed
soldiers drawn from widely different backgrounds whose only concern was to preserve their state.

The divisions that had separated members of the Committee in the
early days in Paris were again apparent now that they were in power.
At first the liberal party dominated the new Parliament and, under the
popular Grand Viziers Said Pasha and Kamil Pasha, a venerated
elder statesman, a policy of Ottomanization was pursued. It was not
long before the well-intentioned efforts of the more moderate
liberals were undone by trouble in the Balkans. The seizure of

33   The euphoria accompanying the proclamation of a constitution in 1908 could not disguise Enver Bey's lack of interest in anything but power

Bosnia-Herzogovina by Austria, the declaration of Bulgarian independence, the union of Crete with Greece, and finally the opposition to the Ottomans in 1912 of the newly formed Balkan League, did not augur well for a decentralized empire. Pressure of events played into the hands of the more militant and extreme members of the Committee. In 1909 a Panislamic revolt with the battle-cry: 'The *Sharia* is in danger, we want the *Sharia*' justified the intervention of an 'army of deliverance' from Salonika, while the new Sultan Mehmed Resad (1909–18) was wholly dependent on the Committee of Union and Progress. For the next two years the Committee had unrivalled power and concentrated their efforts on the Turkish elements of the population. In February 1912, they organized the 'big stick election' in which only six opposition members out of a total of 275 were returned to Parliament. Official opposition to the Committee became impossible so their opponents went underground. In the early summer of 1912, a new opposition group known as the 'Saviour Officers' ousted the Committee and enforced a change of government. No sooner had they

34 Early elections (1909). The polling-place
is the court of a mosque in Constantinople and
the area is surrounded by soldiers

brought Italy, who had been trying to wrest Tripoli from the Turk, to
peace on 17 October than war with the Balkans broke out the very
next day. In January 1913 Enver Bey and the Committee staged a
second coup and, marching into the office of the Minister of War,
Nazim Pasha, Enver shot him dead. The exigencies of war could now
be used as an excuse to keep in power the military triumvirate of
Enver, Talat, and Kemal Pashas.

Enver became War Minister in 1913. Talat served as Minister of
the Interior and after 1916 as Grand Vizier, and Kemal was Military
Governor of Constantinople and Minister of the Navy. Either
divisions within their ranks or the constant pressure of war prevented
this military triumvirate from adopting a policy of radical reform.
The *Sharia* remained untouched as did the Millet system. The young
Turks were unable to pander to nationalist movements among subject peoples and keep the empire strong, so they followed an uneasy
middle way. None the less the relaxation of censorship and recognition of a change in role for women pointed towards a more rational
future and proved a useful base upon which Mustafa Kemal could
build up his Turkish Republic after the war. This was the legacy of
the Young Turks.

8 From Berlin to Sarajevo: The Balkan Threat

THE THIRTY YEARS after the Congress of Berlin were to witness the division of Europe into the two hostile camps of Austria-Hungary and Germany faced by the three Powers of the Triple Entente, Britain, France, and Russia. Events within the Ottoman Empire, if not the sole cause of this division, certainly heightened the tensions between these two groups, provoking finally the outbreak of the Great War and the disintegration of the Ottoman Empire. On the whole, the Turks played an ignominious part in this process. Under the rule of Sultan Abdul Hamid they staggered from one crisis to another, alienating their allies and making no new ones. After the Young Turk revolution of 1908, the hopes of the idealists were dissipated in illusory notions of Panislamism and Pan-Turanianism. But for the emergence of Mustafa Kemal, even the catastrophes of the Great War might well have delayed still further the comparatively belated emergence of Turkish nationalism.

The military dictatorship of Enver Bey was to prove just as pliable in the hands of the Great Powers as the incompetent despotism of Sultan Abdul Hamid. In their defence, the extent of the problems facing the Turkish rulers was immense. The knot of Balkan politics had merely been pulled tighter by the signatories of Berlin. The vexed question of control of the Straits was still the nerve centre of Russian foreign policy. Before long the cry of Arab nationalism would be raised in the southern half of the Ottoman Empire. Neither Britain nor France could afford to see the *status quo* in the Near East upset: for both had a vested interest in the Suez Canal and the future of Egypt, to name but one area of mutual concern. Germany too, with her increasing investment in the railways of the East, brought a new factor to bear on the situation. Meanwhile, on the periphery, Italy, obsessed by her new-found nationalism, was determined to have her pound of flesh if the Ottoman Empire was to be carved up.

It is difficult to credit Sultan Abdul Hamid or his government

35   The Kaiser Franz Joseph at the opening of
the Suez Canal, 17 November 1869. Railways, rather
than canals, fostered the later Turkish-German *entente*

with a foreign policy. Such desultory attempts as he made to appeal
to the Panislamic loyalties of his Muslim subjects won him scant
allegiance and alienated still further his Christian subjects. It also
encouraged the belief in Britain, the Porte's traditional ally, that the
empire was no longer worth saving. In the immediate aftermath of
Berlin, the Sultan proved deliberately obstructive towards the settlement of the Montenegrin and Greek frontiers. His personal antipathy
towards Gladstone was fully reciprocated by the great Liberal
statesman who said that 'the mind of the Sultan who *is* the Turkish
Government, is a bottomless pit of fraud and falsehood and he will
fulfil *nothing* except under force or the proximate threat of force'.
The British occupation of Egypt in 1882 did nothing to improve
their relations.

The British government was becoming increasingly alarmed by
events in Egypt where the Suez Canal, completed in 1869, provided
a vital link to her empire in the East. The liberal rule of Khedive Said
(1854–63) and his successor Ismail (1863–79) had led to the extension
of foreign concessions at a time when Egypt's national finances were
rapidly diminishing. In 1876, Ismail declared Egypt bankrupt.
Loans could be raised only by offering 30 per cent interest while

tribute still had to be paid to the Sultan. This mounting financial crisis led to foreign intervention to control the Egyptian debt – the 'Caisse de la Dette Publique' – which in turn was followed by a nationalist uprising led by Arabi, the Minister of War. With the Khedive's government tottering, a conference was summoned at Constantinople in the summer of 1882. The prevarications of the Sultan prevented any solution to the problem and British and French warships appeared off Alexandria. An Egyptian mob murdered forty Europeans in the streets and Gladstone's government was forced to take action. On 13 September an English force destroyed an Egyptian army at Tel el-Kebir and the forty years of British domination in Egypt had begun. By an Anglo-Turkish Convention signed in 1887, the Sultan agreed to a British occupation of three years with an in-definite right to re-enter the country in the event of any domestic disorder. Such an extension of British influence in Egypt was resented by Russia and France; but the British were unlikely to relinquish the control they had won. The Sultan was in no position to object but his inclination towards Germany – German engineers had been strengthening the fortifications round the Dardanelles – made more imperative the need for an understanding between Russia and Britain in the Near East.

To some extent Britain and Russia were brought closer together by the celebrated massacre of the Armenians by Sultan Abdul Hamid. At the end of the nineteenth century there were about 1 million Armenians under Ottoman rule; but with no one *vilayet* (province) in the empire having an Armenian majority, they were very much an oppressed minority. Tension between the Armenians and their Turkish overlords increased towards the end of the century with the gradual emergence of Armenian national feeling. The Sultan, alarmed by this, created irregular units made up chiefly of Kurds and known as *Hamidiyeh* regiments. In 1894, the large-scale slaughter of Armenians living in the Sassun district provoked a horrified re-action in Western Christendom. The British, full of idealistic fervour, were determined to force the Sultan to mend his ways and permit more autonomy to the Armenians. The Russians, conscious of the Armenians within their own boundaries, were less attracted to such an idea. In any case, the proposed scheme of reforms issued by the Sultan on 20 October was not worth the paper it was written on.

In the winter of 1895–6 tales of further Armenian massacres filtered out of the empire and Lord Salisbury, the British Prime Minister, discussing the matter with the Tsar Nicholas, told him that the Sultan should be deposed. That the Sultan remained and no international crisis ensued was largely the result of Russian concern at the prospect of international control of the Straits. Little had been achieved for the Armenians but the Sultan's action had once again caused a realignment in the form-up of the Great Powers, this time paving the way for an Anglo-Russian *rapprochement*.

The German connection with the Porte was encouraged through the granting of concessions to build railways. The Powers were all anxious to extend their economic influence in the Near East, but railways raised questions of military importance which could not be ignored. However, it is likely that the concern expressed by the British Press over the building of the Baghdad Railway was out of all proportion to its military significance and merely reflected the mounting hostility against Germany in Britain. Georg von Siemens, the leading German industrialist, made a provisional agreement in 1899 to build a railway from Konieh to Baghdad and thence to the Persian Gulf. Four years later, the Porte granted a firm concession to the German-dominated Baghdad Railway Company, which tried to raise some money for the project in Britain. Mr Balfour, the Prime Minister, and Lord Lansdowne, the Foreign Secretary, wanted to invest in the Company, but feelings against the project ran so high that the German offer was refused. The money was eventually raised in France and building on the railway began, although opposition from the Young Turks and financial difficulties delayed work for several years. By 1913 agreement between the Powers over their respective areas of railway-building seems to have been reached and, as late as June 1914, an Anglo-German pact established that Britain would remove her opposition to the building of the railway provided it stopped at Basra, not the Persian Gulf. For Lord Curzon, as Viceroy of India, had already been quick to emphasize the need to protect British interests round the Persian Gulf and Mesopotamia. In 1914 only about 10 per cent of Germany's total foreign investment was in the Ottoman Empire. None the less, it was doubtless a factor in the Porte's decision to join Germany's side in the Great War.

It was in the Balkans that the most intractable problems still lay

36   The gratuitous murder of over 80,000
Armenians in 1895–6 was provoked by the insistence
of the Great Powers on reforms within Turkey

and here the determination of the Turks to hang on to the last vestiges
of Turkey in Europe bore heavily on the more serious rivalry develop-
ing between Austria and Russia over their extension of influence
in that area. As the fiercely nationalistic Balkan states beheld the
tottering Ottoman Empire to the east, so their mood turned from one
of defence against their former overlords to one of combined aggression which took concrete shape in the Balkan League of 1912. Beset
by their own domestic upheavals, there was, it is true, little the Turks
could do. Their only hope would have been to cut their connection
with Europe and concentrate instead on putting their own house in
order. Yet while they still held on to the idea of retaining a multi-
national empire, such a policy was not feasible.

Bulgaria, after the Congress of Berlin, presented a major threat
to the stability of the Balkans. The fashionable desire for national

The Mightiest Military King in Europe :— "Abd-ul, my beloved friend! let us ratify a pact. Give me my railway and keep all the massacres you want. It is true there are some crackbrains who designate you "Great Assassin," "Sultan Rouge," "Abd-ul the Damned," and what not, but do not let these literary effusions disturb you, the Pen is powerless unless backed by the Might of the Sword, and —
I HAVE MY ARMY."

37   Current fears of blatant and cynical German militarism are lucidly expressed in this cartoon of 1913 depicting the supposed route of the Baghdad Railway

unity prompted a movement for the Union of Bulgaria and Eastern Rumelia. Prince Alexander of Battenberg, who had been created ruler in Bulgaria, was unable to prevent the union in 1885 although he personally was not in favour of it. The Russians were even less pleased. They saw the twin Bulgarias as areas of exclusively Russian influence, which the creation of a strong national state would quickly dispel. The Sultan was quite content to set the wolves howling and accepted Alexander as Governor-General of Eastern Rumelia. However, Alexander's pro-Russian sympathies irritated the Bulgarians who forced his abdication in the summer of 1886. Friction between Russia and Bulgaria continued but the Powers were unwilling to see such a relatively minor question provoke a war. It was already clear that a Russian attack on Bulgaria would not be achieved without Austria-Hungary leaping to her defence; and in Britain, too, there was no hostility to the suggestion of a strong and united Bulgaria free from Russian influence. The election of Ferdinand of Saxe-Coburg as

38 Prince Alexander, ruler of Bulgaria, is
forced to abdicate. He was reinstated eleven
days later but left finally on 9 September 1886

ruler of Bulgaria in July 1887 might have caused a Russian invasion,
but for the alliance between Britain, France, and Italy which was
bent on maintaining the *status quo* in the Balkans. With Bismarck
supporting Austria-Hungary, the Tsar had no alternative but to
climb down and Bulgaria became in fact independent of both Russia
and Turkey. The Russians were not to forget the part played by the
Germans in forcing them to lose face.

Of more immediate concern to the Porte was the future of Macedonia, made up of the Turkish *vilayets* of Kossovo, Monastir, and
Salonika. The population of these provinces was mixed but they
aligned themselves chiefly with the Bulgarians. Feuds between the
Greeks and the Bulgars in Macedonia in the 1890s, culminating in
some bomb outrages in Salonika, led to a meeting of the Great

Powers at Murzsteg, outside Vienna, to decide her future. The Sultan was forced to grant greater autonomy to the different groups and to implement some administrative reforms but here he deliberately dragged his feet. The Powers turned their attention once more to Macedonia in 1908 and proposed that the Governor, though a Turkish subject, should be appointed only with their agreement.

The new government in Constantinople proved no more capable of stemming the tide further west in the Balkan peninsula in Bosnia-Herzogovina. The assassination in 1903 of King Alexander of Serbia led to the succession of the aggressively anti-Austrian and Russophil Peter Karageorgevich. Baron Aehrenthal, now Austrian Foreign Minister, was not prepared to sacrifice what he regarded as an Austrian sphere of influence and after a complicated series of negotiations with Prussia in 1906–7, producing misunderstandings on both sides, Austria-Hungary annexed Bosnia-Herzogovina on 5 October 1908. The Turks accepted the annexation in return for compensation of $2\frac{1}{2}$ million Turkish pounds and Serbia was powerless to resist. Russia, embarrassed by the aftermath of the 1905 revolution, was forced again to accept a rebuff from the Central Powers while Serbia harboured a feeling of resentment against her Austrian neighbour which was eventually to trigger off the Great War.

The creation of the Balkan League of 1912 was inspired by the consummate ease with which Italy detached Tripoli from the empire. With no more justification than that she desired compensation in North Africa in view of the *de facto* protectorate the French had established over Morocco, the Italian government delivered an ultimatum to the Porte on 28 September 1911 whereby the Turks were given twenty-four hours to accept the annexation. They naturally refused and at first the war went badly for the Italians, who tried to bluff the Porte into the cession of Tripoli by threatening to attack Salonika, the Straits, and the Syrian coast. The Russians promptly tried to use the war to advance their hold on the Straits but were checked by the British. The bombardment by the Italians of the two fortresses on the Dardanelles caused the Porte to close them to all shipping, while the Italian occupation of the Dodecanese persuaded the Turks to sue for peace at Ouchy on 15 October 1912 where they added Tripoli and 'temporarily' the Dodecanese to Italy. Already the Balkan states, taking a leaf out of the Italian book, had prepared the

39   Tsar Nicholas II (centre) with the King
and Crown Prince of Roumania at Constanza
in 1910

ground for battle. In the spring and summer of 1912, the alliance had
been formed. First Serbia allied with Bulgaria and soon Greece and
Montenegro joined in, although all with very different aims. On 8
October 1912 Montenegro declared war on the Porte and the First
Balkan War had begun.

The Turks were in no position to withstand the onslaught. The
little state of Montenegro, whose ruler, King Nicholas, was probably
only angling for leadership of the Southern Slavs, was a less serious
threat than Serbia and Bulgaria whose armies outnumbered the
Turks and where anti-Turkish feeling was so rampant that their

40 Bulgarian troops and a transport column
pass through a Serbian town during their
ill-fated campaign of 1913

governments could not have prevented the outbreak of war, even
though the Great Powers wished them to. In July 1912 the Young
Turk Cabinet led by Said Pasha was forced to resign and Turkish
military set-backs quickly followed. By the end of October the Turkish army, beaten by both Serbs and Bulgars, was falling back on
Constantinople and was only just able to hold the Chataldja lines,
protecting the capital. They had little alternative but to sign an
armistice with their victors on 3 December. The attitude of the
Powers was as usual one of despair at this upsetting of peace in the
Balkans. Count Berchtold, the new Austrian Foreign Minister, had no
wish to see Serbia gain a foothold on the Adriatic and suggested
instead the formation of an independent state of Albania. Russia
saw the defeat of the Turks as opening the door to an extension of
Bulgaria which she could not contemplate and thus called for an
international convention to discuss the issues. An ambassadorial
conference opened in London in which all that was agreed was that

41 Mechanized transport must have been something of a mixed blessing to the Bulgarian force invading Serbia in 1913

Constantinople and the Straits should remain in Turkish hands while an independent state of Albania should be created. The settlement of a peace was rudely interrupted, however, by Enver Bey's overthrow of the short-lived Liberal régime in Constantinople and the resumption of hostilities by the Turks. The Bulgars and the Serbs replied by taking Adrianople, while Crete surrendered quietly to the Greeks. By the Treaty of London, 30 May 1913, the Turks were forced to cede all their Balkan possessions west of a line from Enos to Midia. The fate of Albania and the Greek islands was to be decided at a later date.

By now the inevitable divisions had appeared in the Balkan front. Roumania had entered the fray and demanded more than just Silistria from Bulgaria. Serbia and Bulgaria were beginning to quarrel about their relative contributions to the war; while Greece and Bulgaria disputed possession of Salonika. The Bulgarians, threatened by Serbia and Greece, launched an unsuccessful attack against the Serbs

42   Sultan Abdul Hamid is forced to accept the
changes inherent in the constitutional revolution
of 1908 when he addresses members of the
Balkan Committee

in June 1913. With the Greeks in Thrace and the Roumanians
occupying the Dobrudja and Sofia, the Turks used the divisions
among their enemies to take back Adrianople. By the resulting Treaty
of Bucharest, 10 August 1913, Macedonia was divided between Serbia
and Greece with Serbia securing part of the Sanjak of Novibazar.
The Sultan was confirmed in his possession of Adrianople by the
Treaty of Constantinople, 29 September 1913.

Out of this tangled skein of events, the defeat of Austria-Hungary,
which had backed Bulgaria in an effort to restrain Serbia, emerged
most clearly. Russia, as ever bent on control of the Straits, had considered early in 1913 using the Balkan War as a pretext for seizing the

Straits by force. The weakness of her Black Sea navy decided her against it. For the Turks, the war had pushed them further into the German camp and it was likely that under Enver Bey, who had served as Military Attaché in Berlin, the trend would continue. The appointment of the German soldier Liman von Sanders to command the Turkish First Army Corps in Constantinople had so irritated the Russians that he was eventually created Inspector-General of the Turkish Army in a face-saving operation that in no way obscured worsening Russo-German relations. As the year 1914 dawned the Powers had withdrawn into their respective camps. There were, of course, other causes of this division than those discussed here. It is significant, however, that the assassination of the Archduke Francis Ferdinand, heir to the Hapsburg throne, on 28 June 1914 in Sarajevo was the work of Serbian extremists. The origins of Serbia and her struggle for independence are all part of the same story; moreover one in which the Ottomans found themselves intimately involved. When the armies of the Great Powers started surging forward to do battle, the Turks were faced with the awkward decision of whether to join in or stay neutral. The decision to side with the Germans spelt the end of the Ottoman Empire; it saw also the rise of the Turkish Republic.

9 Out of Defeat, Victory

IT WOULD BE impossible to separate from the history of these years the career of the one man capable of turning defeat into victory. Mustafa Kemal was to use the Ottoman defeat in the Great War to enhance his own military prestige and to foment the latent feelings of nationalism buried deep in Anatolia.

Born in 1881 in Salonika, Mustafa Kemal was brought up in a garrison town and naturally tended towards a military career. At the age of twenty-two he graduated from military college and was posted to a cavalry regiment in Damascus. Although he played no important part in the Young Turk revolt of 1908, he was heavily involved in the café politics of the time and even then was distinguished from his fellow officers, many of whom were mere military adventurers, by his singleness of purpose and patriotism. The Balkan wars gave him valuable military experience and when Turkey entered the Great War he was serving as Ottoman Military Attaché at Sofia.

The Turkish decision to enter the war was a vexed one for Enver Bey and one that Mustafa Kemal opposed. Respect for German military efficiency inclined Enver Bey towards joining the Germans but it was the requisitioning by Britain of two warships that were being built in private British shipyards that finally tipped the scales. Germany promptly sold two warships, the *Goeben* and the *Breslau*, to Turkey to make up for the loss and when the Porte allowed these ships to bombard the Russian Black Sea ports, there was no turning back. By 5 November all the Entente Powers had declared war on Turkey. Neither the attempts by Enver to mobilize the entire Islamic world by declaring a *jihad* or Holy War against the Entente Powers, nor his appeal to Pan-Turanianism, an effort to unite all Turkish-speaking peoples, was to meet with any success. The illogicality of the Turkish position was all too evident, for if her enemies were infidels so too were her allies, and the British were quick to encourage the Arab revolt by reminding the Arabs of the dangers of Turcification.

43 Mustafa Kemal (Atatürk). His qualities of leadership and powers of organization were revealed not only at Gallipoli but also in his controlled withdrawal on the Eastern front during the Great War

Mustafa Kemal was to win his spurs by successfully thwarting the Gallipoli landings of April 1915. This established him firmly as the military idol that Turkey so badly needed. With utter disregard for his own personal safety and by pitting his faith in the courage of the Mehmedjk (the Turkish 'Tommy Atkins'), Kemal not only achieved victory over the Allies at the battles for Chunuk Bair and Anafarta, but organized a successful counter-attack that was to lead to the British evacuation. The battle for Chunuk Bair was crucial for two reasons. By holding it successfully against the Allied attack, Mustafa Kemal removed the threat of immediate Turkish collapse and the fall of Constantinople. Secondly, the battle provided him with the opportunity to demonstrate to the Turks his indomitable courage and military skill. He recognized the opportunity and grasped it eagerly. By doing so he created a legendary aura about himself, without which his later actions would have been impossible. Chunuk Bair is the mountain that dominates the Gallipoli peninsula. Mustafa Kemal recognized at once that control of these heights was essential. Desperately short of men, he ordered extra reinforcements without waiting for permission from his commander Liman von Sanders. He remained in the thick of battle as the Australians surged up the hillside. After nearly a week of fighting he told his men:

> The enemy must be forced into the sea. To achieve this you will fight to the end. You will fight to the last soldier. You will die rather than cede one centimetre of ground.

When their ammunition ran out, the Turks drove the enemy back with their bayonets and their hands. In his diary Mustafa Kemal wrote later:

> They had such calmness, and such confidence in God that I envied them. These men are the heroes of the war. They witness the deaths of their friends, and they accept the knowledge that their own hour has come. No tremor in their hands, a look of exaltation. Who, save God, can read the mind of a man. . . ? I am humbled by their nobility.

The advantage gained was soon to be dissipated by the fruitless campaigns pursued by the Turks against the Russians on the Eastern front, where Enver Bey was indulging in fanciful dreams of re-creating an Asiatic empire. Insanely jealous of Kemal, he packed him off to the Caucasian front where, despite Turkish defeats, Kemal captured the east Anatolian towns of Mush and Bitlis. He was rewarded for his efforts with the Medal of the Golden Sword – hardly the extent of his ambitions. With the coming of the Russian revolution in 1917, the Russian front crumbled and Kemal was promptly appointed Commander of the Seventh Ottoman Army, whose job was to evacuate the Arab provinces in the face of the relentless advance of General Allenby.

The Arab revolt, which had broken out in Mecca in June 1916 under the aegis of Sharif Husain, had gathered strength with the appearance of the Egyptian Expeditionary Force of General Allenby,

44   Turkish prisoners in a cage after the Third
Battle of Krithia on 4 June 1915 at the height of
the Gallipoli campaign

which did more to drain the Turkish resistance than the romantic
exploits of Colonel T. E. Lawrence in blowing up the Hejaz Railway.
In March 1917 Baghdad fell to the British and in November Allenby
broke through Turkish lines between Beersheba and Gaza. In
December he took Jerusalem, the Christmas present for which Lloyd
George had asked. Kemal, dogged by ill-health, was away from the
Eastern campaign until the final offensive in the summer of 1918.
Refusing to fight for either Damascus or Aleppo, he retreated head-
long with what was left of the Turkish army, intent only on securing
the southern frontier of Anatolia. This he achieved and when the

45 The Kaiser, the Sultan, and Enver Bey,
ride through the streets of Constantinople
in 1907

Turkish delegate, Rauf, signed the armistice with Admiral Calthorpe at Mudros, Mustafa Kemal was the only Turkish commander to have served his country for four years without suffering a single defeat.

By 1918 the empire had ceased to exist. With the collapse of the Bulgarian front the Allies, based on Salonika, threatened Constantinople. The British forces had overrun the Arab world; effectively all that remained of the empire was a central fragment in Asia Minor. It was not as if the government in Constantinople had sufficient kudos to bargain with the Allies for the return of some of her lost territories. Mehmed V. Resad, the Sultan whom Enver had pushed into the war, had died on 23 July 1918; he was followed by his brother Vahid-ed Din, who observed to the Sheikh of Islam as he mounted the throne: 'I am at a loss. Pray for me.' The discredited trio of Enver, Talat, and Kemal had fled across the Black Sea in a German gunboat and the Committee of Union and Progress was finished. Two of the Sultan's earlier acts could hardly have encouraged the Nationalists. He dissolved the Parliament and in February 1919 appointed his brother-in-law, Damad Ferid, Grand Vizier. Ferid was loathed by the Nationalists but favoured by the Allies who realized he would offer little resistance to their schemes for partition. The final weakness in the Ottoman position lay in the Allied commitment to a number of secret agreements concerning the partition of the empire made throughout the course of the war. The Bolshevik government in Russia renounced all Tsarist agreements, but as Arnold Toynbee has put it: 'like wolves about the camp fire the Powers were prowling at the threshold with hungry eyes, for Turkey by nature is sick, and imperialism is greedy'. As if the avarice of Britain, France, and Italy was not enough, the negotiations for a settlement had now to take into account the dreams of the Greeks for resurrecting a Hellenic Empire by acquiring an enclave in Asia Minor.

After their peculiarly undistinguished part in the war, the Greeks, again under the leadership of Venizelos, whom Lloyd George regarded as 'the greatest statesman Greece had thrown up since the days of Pericles', based their argument on those very principles of self-determination which President Wilson had decreed should form the basis of the settlement. For, they argued, should not the predominately Greek settlement in Smyrna be afforded protection? Lloyd George, not only on account of his personal admiration for Venizelos but also because he was anxious to forestall the excessive demands of the Italians in the area, was only too happy to support the Greek cause. On 15 May 1919 an army of 20,000 Greek troops landed at Smyrna and in the words of Sir Winston Churchill 'set up their standards of invasion and conquest in Asia Minor'. Halide Edib, who personified the emancipated Turkish female, dressed in black and her face unveiled, addressed a gathering of Turks in one of the squares: 'Brothers, Sisters, Countrymen, Muslims: when the night is darkest and seems eternal, the light of dawn is nearest.' Her message was not lost on the Turkish people. As the Allies ponderously went about their business of drawing up the Sèvres peace terms, they were for the most part happily unaware of the flames that had been kindled in Nationalist hearts by this final affront to their self-esteem. By encouraging the Greeks to invade Smyrna, Lloyd George had made a most disastrous mistake.

Meanwhile, Mustafa Kemal had not been idle. In May 1919 he had been sent as Inspector-General to northern Anatolia. Here, free from the warships of the Allies and the control of the Sultan's government, he was able to use his singular force of personality to bind together not only the army leaders like Ali Fuad Pasha and Kazim Karabekir, but also the soldiers and the peasants of the Anatolian plateau. As the Sultan came to be seen more and more as a puppet of the Allies, so Mustafa Kemal was able to win over to his side the upholders of law and order as well. The Sultan for his part was committed to compliance with the Allied terms and could merely view with misgivings the growth of the Nationalist movement. Certainly the Allies were unlikely to come to his aid for they badly underestimated the forces of nationalism in Turkey. Already Mustafa Kemal had seen the importance of enlisting political as well as military support for his cause and at a conference at Erzerum on 23 July 1919, a 'National Organization' was formed and the principles of the movement were laid down. Two months later a second congress met in the rooms of a secondary school at Sivas. An emissary of President Wilson, General J. G. Harbord attended the congress and could not fail to be impressed with the determination of the representatives. He left with the words of Kemal humming in his ears:

> If we can't succeed, rather than fall into the palm of the enemy like a bird, and be condemned to a gradual, ignoble death, we prefer, being the sons of our forefathers, to die fighting.

After these two congresses, Kemal's leadership of the movement was assured beyond doubt. With the Sultan's government now in a quite untenable position, Damad Ferid had little alternative but to resign on 1 October 1919. As a gesture of conciliation, the Sultan appointed a pro-Nationalist Cabinet led by Field-Marshal Ali Riza and a new Parliament in December 1919 showed a Kemalist majority. By now Kemal had moved his headquarters to Angora, the site of modern Ankara, where a National Pact was drawn up, and it was perfectly clear that the Nationalist government would not accept the Allied peace terms. To the Allies, the Nationalists were becoming more and more outrageous in their exploits, one of which was to seize

46 Venizelos, Prime Minister of Greece, in
London in 1921. He launched the Greek invasion
of Turkey, which so inspired Turkish national feeling

in January 1920 an ammunition dump under the guard of the French
in the Gallipoli peninsula and remove it to Asia Minor. On 16 March
the Allies moved into Constantinople and proceeded to purge the
Turkish Parliament. Rauf and Kara Vasif were arrested and about 150
Nationalist deputies forced to resign. On 12 April, the Sultan dissolved the Parliament.

With the occupation of Constantinople the British had once more
played into Mustafa Kemal's hands. Many of the Parliamentary
deputies fled to Angora and on 23 April a reconstructed Parliament
there began its first session as the Great National Assembly of
Turkey.

By this time, the original declaration of the Nationalists to stand
by the Sultanate and the Caliphate was beginning to wear a little thin.
Mustafa Kemal was confirmed as Commander-in-Chief and President and the importance of the Assembly lay in its establishment of an
organizational frame-work with which ultimately to build the Turkish

Republic. Furthermore, by the law of Fundamental Organization 'it was stated that Sovereignty belonged to the people fully and no longer lay in the hands of a single monarchial individual'. The days of the Sultanate were numbered.

While Mustafa Kemal had been mobilizing resistance to the Allied demands and creating the Nationalist organization in Anatolia, the Allies had been preparing the draft of a peace treaty. The delay of nearly two years between the signing of the armistice at Mudros and the drafting of the terms of a peace treaty was by no means the result solely of the intransigence of the Nationalists. It should be borne in mind that the Allies were busy hammering out a settlement for Germany and the Balkans and that their attempts to solve the Ottoman problem were bedevilled by the arguments that arose over the whole question of mandated territories. President Wilson, armed with his fourteen points, found that the American people were becoming less and less enamoured of the whole Eastern question and they refused to give him the support for which he asked. Quarrels had broken out between the British and the French on the question of their respective spheres of influence, so it was not altogether surprising that the final settlement was delayed. Conferences had been held in London in the early part of 1920 and a further meeting was held at San Remo in April. The settlement, when it came, was draped in the flags of Western imperialism. The Treaty of Sèvres can be regarded as the third British error, although the other Allies must bear some of the responsibility. By the treaty, the Arab provinces, to the loss of which the Sultan and the Nationalists were resigned, were handed over to the Mandatories. Armenia and Kurdistan in the East were to become autonomous states. Smyrna and the rich lands of south-west Anatolia would go to Italy. Constantinople was to remain Turkish but the area of the Straits was to come under a mixed Allied Commission. The whole of Thrace was to be handed over to the hated Greeks, who would also acquire eight Turkish islands in the Aegean. Much of Anatolia itself was to fall under the sphere of influence of France and Italy. The date of the signature of the treaty was heralded as a day of national mourning throughout Turkey.

The blunders of the British government had left them now in a position where they could exercise less and less influence on events

47   Mustafa Kemal's dictatorial treatment of
the Assembly indicated his impatience with any
constitutional check on his personal power

in Turkey. The final outcome was to depend on whether the Turks could withstand the Greek onslaught; and if they did whether they could expel the Greeks from the mainland. The first Greek offensive, authorized by the Allies, began in June 1920. Successful round the Sea of Marmora and in capturing Adrianople from the Turks, the Greeks were able at first to benefit from their superior material resources and the fact that the Turks were bottled up in the centre of Anatolia. Not only this, but an anti-Nationalist uprising in the Brusa area led by the Circassian, Ahmed Anzevuz, and supported by the Constantinople government, added to Mustafa Kemal's difficulties. Even so, the Greeks were surprised by the fierce resistance of the Turkish irregulars and their inability to penetrate further into the centre of Anatolia led to a conference of the interested parties held in London in February 1921. Although offered concessions, the Kemalist Turks refused to give in and by May 1921 the Allies left the Turks and the Greeks to sort out their own differences.

48 Camels that have carried Turkish military
equipment from the Sakarya River to the west
coast rest in a street in Smyrna

The Greeks without Allied support were a less formidable foe.
In addition, Mustafa Kemal was helped by a satisfactory resolution
of the Eastern boundary question due to the signing of a treaty at
Moscow with Stalin on 16 March 1921, by which the Soviets gained
Kars and Ardahan. The Russo-Turkish boundary in the Caucasus has
remained until this day and revealed how traditional Russo-Turkish
enmity could be submerged if only by their common hostility to the
Treaty of Sèvres. Certainly there was little ideological unity between
the optimistic Communists of the new Soviet Republic and the
sceptical Turkish Nationalists.

When the Greeks launched their second offensive in March 1921,
they were confronted by a much more disciplined army than the
collection of irregulars who had fought them a year earlier. The

49 General Papoulas, Crown Prince George,
and General Stratigos during the Greek
offensive in Anatolia in 1921

campaign was directed towards Eskishehir and Afyon Karahisar,
both important railway junctions. They took Afyon Karahisar but
were unable to occupy Eskishehir after being turned back in the
valley of Inönü by a Turkish army under Ismet. Undismayed, the
Greeks launched a new offensive on 10 July 1921 and this time, after
bombarding Eskishehir for ten days, forced Ismet to evacuate it.
Soon would come the moment for which Mustafa Kemal had long
been preparing.

The Greeks now set their sights on Angora and it was evident to
both sides that here lay the key to victory. The Greek Press waxed
lyrical about the prospect of repeating the conquests of Alexander the
Great. The Turks retiring towards Angora took up a defensive position round the river Sakarya. Mustafa Kemal conducted operations

himself. For twenty-two days and nights in the longest pitched battle in history, fortunes ebbed and flowed. No sooner had the Greeks pierced the sixty-mile-long front, than Mustafa Kemal ordered reserves to plug up the gap. In the end it was the Greeks who broke first. Although their army retreated in good order to Smyrna, there was no denying the importance of the engagement. Mustafa Kemal was endowed with the honorific Muslim title of *Ghazi*, Destroyer of the Christians. His victory was to prove decisive.

There was still the question of the peace treaty. After Sakarya, the French resolved to cut their losses by a private pact, known as the 'Angora Agreement', in which the British were not consulted. This

50 Smyrna 1922: today the old Greek houses
not destroyed by this raging fire are being
demolished to make way for modern flats   118

revised the boundary line between Syria and Turkey while France agreed to withdraw from Cilicia. Besides infuriating the British, this withdrew from the Greeks yet another plank of support; it signified also the recognition by France of the Nationalist government in Angora as the ruling government of Turkey. The Italians followed suit by quietly retiring from Adalia and reaching a separate agreement with Mustafa Kemal. The Greeks attempted a last throw in the summer of 1922 but the Turkish forces swept them westwards; in any case, they no longer had the stomach to stand their ground. They retreated from Ushaq to Smyrna where the Turks followed them, looting and pillaging as they went. For a week a great fire swept

51 After the great fire of 1922 refugees jostle with each other at the quayside in Smyrna trying to gain passage back to Greece

through the city. The cause of it was unknown but to many Turks it must have seemed the symbolic purging if their fatherland. With the Greeks defeated there remained only the British.

In view of Lloyd George's Turcophobe prejudices it seemed that Mustafa Kemal's intention to push northwards to Constantinople and Adrianople – no more than the stated aims of the National Pact – might be opposed by the British forces at Chanak, situated on the Adriatic shores of the Dardanelles. The danger of an incident sparking off a major battle between the Turks and the British was very real. Mustafa Kemal's demand for the evacuation of the Greeks from eastern Thrace was eventually conceded by the British at the eleventh hour and the crisis was over. Lloyd George promptly resigned. As Lord Kinross has put it: 'The Macedonian had defeated the Celt.' Yet no one realized better than Mustafa Kemal that the hardest part was still in front of him. As he stood watching the smouldering embers of Smyrna he had observed prophetically:

> They think that this is the end, that I have reached my goal. But it is only after this that we shall really begin to do something. It is only now that our real work is beginning.

10 Turkey: A Nation is Born

IT TOOK MUSTAFA KEMAL five years to create the new Republic of Turkey and to silence all effective opposition to his rule. The thread running through all these years of war and reconstruction is his own single-minded drive. Neither in war nor peace would he let himself be side-tracked for a moment from his declared goal of liberating the Turkish people from the shackles of the past. Though a dictator, he was not so in the classic sense. If he dealt with his enemies ruthlessly it was not through motives of personal malice but because they blocked the path he had chosen. He wore the mantle of power carelessly, never obsessed with its trimmings. The pursuit of glory never became an end in itself. His Rabelaisian appetite for drink and women was a distraction that ruined his health, but never deflected his attention from affairs of state. His Constitution was no temporary scaffolding that would collapse after he died, for he built always with an eye to the future. Like Napoleon, he was not born a native of the country he liberated: unlike Napoleon he remained true to his ideals.

Once the Armistice had been signed with the Allies at Mudanya on 11 October 1922, the immediate question to be resolved was the future of the Sultanate. In a sense the Allies had forced this issue into the open by inviting the Sultan, as well as the Nationalists, to send a delegate to the Peace Conference which opened at Lausanne on 20 November. Mustafa Kemal was already convinced that the Sultanate could not be allowed to continue, but he had to tread carefully at first. It was one thing to depose a Sultan – the history of the House of Osman was littered with depositions – but it was quite another to abolish the office itself. Even his closest advisers counselled a more cautious approach. Rauf, no supporter of the Sultan, Vahid-ed Din, could not bring himself to support the abolition. Refet thought that the Sultan should become a constitutional monarch. Ali Faud could not make up his mind. The victorious entry of the Nationalists into Constantinople and the open adulation of the populace for the

swashbuckling Refet, who even preached from the pulpit in Santa
Sofia, went a long way towards massing support behind Mustafa
Kemal. The contrast provided by the feckless Sultan with his intimi-
dated retinue had all the elements of a comic opera. When Refet
demanded the resignation of the Sultan's Cabinet, Vahid-ed Din
foolishly tried to play for time, hoping the Allies would bale him out.
Instead they played once more right into the hands of Mustafa
Kemal. By inviting a delegate from the Sublime Porte to Lausanne
they prepared the ground for abolition, for no representative of the
Sultan any longer represented the real feelings of the Turks. Mustafa
Kemal steam-rollered the Assembly in Angora where there was
strong opposition to his proposal. He cut through the abstruse
arguments of the scholarly defendants of the Sultanate with a
soldier's simplicity:

MAP NO. 5
The Balkans in 1923

Sovereignty and the Sultanate are taken by strength, by power, and by force. It was by force that the sons of Osman seized the sovereignty and Sultanate of the Turkish nation: they have maintained this usurpation for six centuries. Now the Turkish nation has rebelled and put a stop to these usurpers, and has effectively taken sovereignty and Sultanate into its own hands.

This was enough for the Assembly: the Sultanate was declared abolished. On 4 November the last government of the Ottoman

53   Mustafa Kemal (centre) with members of the
Ankara Diplomatic Corps in August 1922 at the
time when Ankara became Turkey's capital

Empire resigned the seals of office to the deposed Sultan. Vahid-ed
Din, bereft of Allied and political support, and terrified for his
personal safety, resolved to flee. On 17 November in the company of a
few eunuchs and personal servants, his jewels packed away in
trunks, he slipped out of the Yildiz Kiosk and boarded H.M.S.
Malaya which took him off to Malta. Happily for the Nationalists
this feeble exit took away from the Sultan much of the political support upon which he might have relied. Sensitive to the religious
sensibilities of the Turks, Mustafa Kemal deliberately retained for
the time being the office of Caliph to which he appointed Prince
Abdul Mejid, the Sultan's cousin and Heir Apparent. Abdul Mejid
was a cultured man of some distinction and known for his sympathy
towards the Nationalists. His authority was nevertheless rigidly

124

54   Mustafa Kemal inspects his troops during the campaign against the Greeks in 1922

curtailed by the Great National Assembly and there was no question of his exercising any temporal power. Thus in the space of less than one month Mustafa Kemal had overthrown a system of government that had lasted without a break since 1288.

Delegates of the Great Powers were by now converging on Lausanne. Very much against his own will, Ismet had been dispatched there by Mustafa Kemal to go and do battle with the lions of European diplomacy. Despite his acute sense of inferiority, he acquitted himself with distinction and in the event most of the Turkish demands were met. It was certainly a complex business. Not only was there the question of the frontiers but also explosive issues such as control of the Straits and the foreign Capitulations all of which had to be resolved. It would take six months for any agreement to be reached on the terms of the general Peace Treaty; and with the

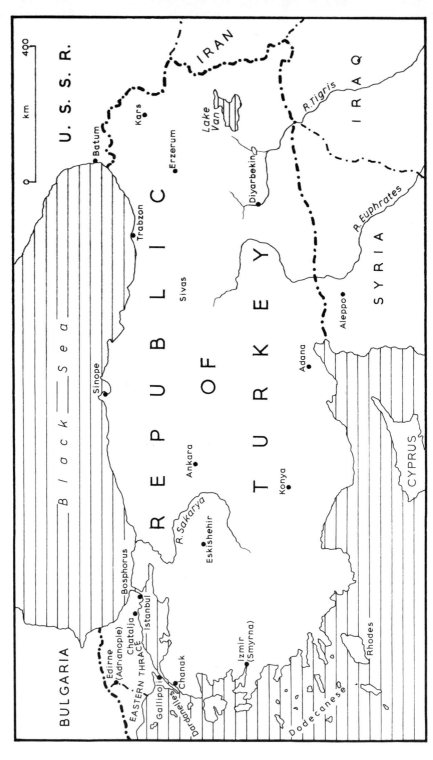

MAP No. 6 The Republic of Turkey in 1923

treaty came eighteen conventions, agreements, declarations, and protocols, as well as six exchanges of letters. It was in December that the question of the Straits was discussed. Chicherin, the Russian delegate, harangued the conference in his squeaky voice. His diatribe disclosed an interesting volte-face in Russian policy. Hitherto the traditional Russian line had been to try and control the Straits in order to allow her navy access into the Mediterranean; now Russia wanted to close them to all foreign powers except Turkey so that her Black Sea coast was not vulnerable to attack. Chicherin, however, had bargained without the Turkish Nationalists. They had no wish to see the Black Sea became a focus of Russo-Turkish friction and instead supported the Allied suggestion of an International Straits Commission to be established at Constantinople. The Soviet government could not bring itself to sign an agreement. The Turkish position was to be vindicated finally at the Convention of Montreux (1936) when the Turks were given sole guardianship of the Straits with the right to fortify them.

The problem of foreign Capitulations was more difficult. This was a patronizing relationship that often led to foreign abuse and could not be tolerated any longer by the Nationalists. Already before the war they had declared the Capitulations formally abolished but on the resumption of peace the foreign powers sought to re-establish their privileged position within the empire. When Ismet made clear the Turkish intention to abolish the Capitulations, Lord Curzon opposed his suggestion and the Conference broke down in February 1923. Two months later, Curzon, recognizing the steely determination of the Turks on this point, gave way in the interests of achieving the rest of the settlement. The French, who had considerable economic interests within the empire, suffered most.

So far as the territorial provisions of the treaty went, it was agreed that Turkey should recover the whole of Anatolia, western Thrace as far as the river Maritza, which included Constantinople and Adrianople, and the islands of Imbros and Tenedos. A much-disputed provision was the absorption of the Kurdish *vilayet* of Mosul into the British-dominated kingdom of Iraq. Kurdish revolts were to break out subsequently but the treaty effectively put an end to the possibility of an autonomous Kurdish state. The most Draconian measure of all was the compulsory exchange of Christians in

Turkey for Muslims in Greece. Hundreds of thousands of people were forced to leave their homes to remove the chance of religious friction in the future. It was logical, if inhuman. With the Capitulations went the Millet system too.

The Treaty of Lausanne stands out from all the other peace treaties between the Turks and the European powers during the preceding century. However unpalatable it may have been, the Allies were forced to accept the new-found determination of the Turks. Lord Curzon may have complained about Ismet's oft-repeated phrase 'sovereignty, sovereignty, sovereignty', but he was the first to recognize that anything less than full sovereignty at home would have spelt the end of the Nationalist government. If the Allies wanted a settlement they would have to accept this even if it meant the reluctant granting of concessions. This had to be a treaty based on fact not artificial theories. The Turks would not squander their unusual advantage by asking too much; but again they would not be dictated to over questions about which they had already made up their minds. It was this above all which lent some permanence to the settlement.

While the conference had been deliberating at Lausanne, Mustafa Kemal had been laying the foundations of the first real political party in modern Turkey – the People's Party. In the spring of 1923, the Great National Assembly dissolved itself and in June 286 deputies were elected to a new chamber which first sat in August. The Assembly elected Mustafa Kemal as President of the Republic and as its first major act it ratified the Treaty of Lausanne. By 2 October, the last Allied troops had left Constantinople and on 9 October Ismet Pasha moved at a meeting of the People's Party that 'Ankara is the seat of Government of the Turkish State.' On 29 October came the most dramatic utterance of all. In a draft amendment prepared by Mustafa Kemal it was declared that:

55 Mustafa Kemal instructs teachers in the change from the Arabic to the Latin alphabet in 1928

56 Kemal worked ceaselessly to liberate women from the shackles of Islamic custom

128

. . . the form of government of the State of Turkey is a Republic . . . the President of Turkey is elected by the Great National Assembly in plenary session from among its own members . . . The President of Turkey is the Head of the State . . . and appoints the Prime Minister.

Throughout the country the news of the proclamation was celebrated with the salute of 101 guns. Under the guise of parliamentary democracy, Mustafa Kemal had become a dictator. Compared by an admiring comrade to the Holy Trinity itself, Kemal admitted, 'It is true but don't tell anyone.'

Was Mustafa Kemal trying to deceive the Turks as to his real intentions? Perhaps, for he already had in mind measures for more radical reforms than he could have revealed but for the dictatorial powers he had assumed. As a French nineteenth-century observer remarked when asked for his remedy for Turkey's problems: 'Ouvrez

57   Ataturk during military manœuvres at Smyrna in the 1930s. The birth of the Turkish Republic helped restore self-respect to her soldiers

les femmes, fermez le Coran.' It was in this direction that Mustafa Kemal moved.

By far the most profound departure from the past was the abolition of the Caliphate in April 1924. Using the occasion of a call by two Indians, the Aga Khan and Amir Ali, to preserve the Caliphate, Mustafa Kemal mobilized the still potent xenophobia of the Turk to move its abolition in the Assembly. The Bill was passed and the Caliph bundled off unceremoniously to Bulgaria. Along with the Caliph went the Sheikh of Islam, the *Sharia*, and the *Evkâf*. The tentative moves of the earlier reformers were superseded by a root and branch separation of church and state. That so radical a break with the past was possible at all was chiefly because of the political and military power of Mustafa Kemal; it was also made possible by the support of the women who saw in this move their emancipation from the shackles of Muslim law.

The abolition of the last vestiges of Islam did indeed make necessary its replacement by a new system of law. In March 1921, a Turkish Civil Code, virtually a translation of the Swiss Civil Code, was promulgated. By this the practice of polygamy, divorce at the husband's behest, inequality of women's shares in the division of estates were all abolished. Soon after this, a new commercial code and a new penal code were added. In 1928, the Assembly removed from the Constitution any reference to Islam as the official religion of the state. As the Arab-based religion vanished from Turkey, so too did the Arabic alphabet. Mustafa Kemal sought also to harness social customs borrowed from the West to his new secular state. Sporting a Panama himself, he cajoled the Turks into replacing the traditional fez with the European hat. Even more radical was his removal of the veil, symbolic somehow of their subjection, from Turkish women. By 1935 emancipation of women had gone so far that seventeen were elected deputies to the Great National Assembly. In the same year, he made surnames compulsory. Before, the Arab nomenclature had existed and people with the same name were distinguished from each other by their trade (for instance, Ali the gardener, Bostanci Ali). Mustafa Kemal felt that such a clumsy system should be removed and by 1 January 1935 everyone had to choose a surname. The nation conferred on him the name Atatürk (Father Turk). Education and service to the state became the yardstick of success. A new

58   A post-war photograph of the
Galata Koprusu, one of the two

bureaucratic élite, fashioned to suit Atatürk's requirements, came to
dominate the country. Much of what he tried to do extended no
further than the towns but this in no way detracts from the importance
of what he had started.

Mustafa Kemal, of course, was unable to effect all these reforms
without provoking fierce opposition. Even when he was still the
popular hero in 1923, there were 100 deputies who abstained from
voting when he was elected President. Under Rauf, a Progressive
Party sprang up which based its appeal on a purer form of democracy
than that of the People's Party. It proved obstructive to Mustafa

132

bridges over the Golden Horn in
Istanbul

Kemal in the Assembly but its opposition was soon to be eclipsed by
the more serious revolt of the Kurds in eastern Anatolia, which was
directed against the reforming policy of Mustafa Kemal's government, particularly the abolition of the Caliphate. The rebellion united
the Turks behind Mustafa Kemal, who used it as an excuse to pass
through the Assembly a statute of Law and Order giving him virtually dictatorial powers. The Kurdish ring-leaders were rounded up
and executed but Mustafa Kemal had bigger fish to fry.

In 1926 the revelation of a plot to murder him led to the setting up
of Trials for Treason. To these were summoned not only twenty-five

deputies but also his old comrades of the early Nationalist days Refet, Ali Fuad, and Rauf. The generals were spared but many were liquidated. Mustafa Kemal had no further need to resort to such methods, reminiscent of the worst of the Sultans. For, from then on there was effectively no opposition. It is difficult to explain this departure from his professed democratic rule, still less to justify it. He was fond of saying 'the Peasant is our Master' and was to claim that he behaved in this way because 'it was the people that I was afraid of'. Probably he was most afraid of the forces of the unknown, of the mystical side of Islam that he never claimed to understand. Whatever the motives, the incident was both unfortunate and unnecessary. It detracts in no small way from his achievement.

Although there were times when he strengthened his dictatorship in the face of political opposition, it cannot be denied that he deliberately encouraged the growth of parliamentary government and a free judiciary based on Western models. To begin with, there had been an increasing feeling in Turkey that the hostility of Europe placed the Turks in the same camp as the Russians, and superficially Lenin's assumption of power bears some comparison with that of Mustapha Kemal. Yet Kemal held no brief for Communism, and his conviction that the Turks placed great store by free institutions proved well founded. This was the true measure of his success. It is for this that he is remembered as the founder of modern Turkey which for all its vicissitudes has emerged as a comparatively free modern state in a notoriously unstable part of the world.

The drawing of lines in history is necessarily a very arbitrary business but in some measure it may be held that the later career of Mustafa Kemal was merely the logical extension of what he had achieved by 1923. By then the die was cast and Turkey's course was set. The appearance of Turkish Nationalism cannot be simply explained; it came as the result of too many different influences. Always the target for Russian expansion, the Ottomans were dragged into the maelstrom of Balkan and Arab politics where the seeds of independence were being sown throughout the nineteenth century. The revolution in communications spelled the end of isolationist Turkey. There were too many outside interests involved in the remnants of her empire for her to side-step the decision whether to rationalize and cut her losses or stagger blindly on.

59 Ataturk's special train – built in Germany
in 1935 by order of the Turkish Government

At the end of the day, four men stand out from the course of Ottoman history like signposts pointing the way to the Republic of 1923:
Sultan Mahmud, Namik Kemal, Enver Bey, and Mustafa Kemal.
Where the Sultan began to reform the empire, Namik Kemal
furnished an intellectual argument for bridging the gap between
East and West; where Enver Bey offered the ruthless military leadership essential to make the Young Turk movement a political force,
Mustafa Kemal provided the victories in both war and peace that
set the seal on the Republic. The Marxist historian would doubtless
disagree, but it is difficult to separate the attainment of Turkish
independence from the accident of personalities. It was the Ottoman
sons who created the Turkish fatherland.

Acknowledgements

The author and publishers wish to record their grateful thanks to copyright owners for the use of the illustrations listed below:

Camera Press Ltd. for: 44

Mary Evans Picture Library for: 1, 6, 9, 10, 12, 14, 15, 18, 20, 21, 22, 24, 25, 28, 29, 38

The Mansell Collection for: 36

The National Portrait Gallery, London, for: 19

Paul Popper Ltd. for: 5, 13, 16, 26, 27, 32, 39, 40, 41, 43, 57, 59

The Radio Times Hulton Picture Library for: 7, 11, 17, 30, 31, 35, 37, 46, 48, 49, 50, 51, 53, 54

The Trustees of the British Museum for: 2, 3, 4

Index

138

Printed in Great Britain
by Jarrold and Sons Limited,
Norwich